The Gem Cutter's Handbook

THE GEM CUTTER'S HANDBOOK

2025 Brentwood Press, LLC
P.O. Box 132
Arrington, TN 37014
BrentwoodPress.net
DanLynchGems.com

Cover: Michael Holmes
Layout: Doug Powell and Michael Holmes

ISBN: 978-1-7370578-0-2

Printed in China

10 9 8 7 6 5 4 3 2 1

The Gem Cutter's Handbook

Dan Lynch, GIA GG

Table of Contents

Introduction

As long as I can remember, I've loved gems and minerals. I took my first geology class in college mainly, because I was told it was the easiest way to fulfill my science credit, but that course sparked a more profound fascination with all things rocks. That interest led me to earn my first degree in geology and begin taking trips to collect and dig for specimens.

Fast forward several years: my 10-year-old daughter Sarah and I took a trip to Mount Ida, Arkansas, to participate in the World Championship Crystal Dig. We had such a great time that our mineral-hunting adventures became an annual tradition. Together, we searched for tourmaline in California, sunstone in Oregon, sapphires and rubies in North Carolina, and sapphires in Montana.

It was on one of those Montana trips, after riding horses into the mountains and camping in teepees, that my faceting journey truly began. While digging for sapphires in a nearby river, I met a fellow traveler who was a gem cutter. I spent several days peppering him with questions and listening intently to his insights. I left that trip with a clear desire to learn how to cut gemstones myself.

My first step was ordering a faceting machine, the Graves Mark 4, from one of the familiar ads in Rock & Gem Magazine. While waiting for it to arrive, I attended our local gem and mineral club's annual show and was thrilled to see someone demoing the exact machine I had just purchased. That man was Will Smith. He told me he taught faceting classes with the Middle Tennessee Gem & Mineral Society. I signed up the next day. Will became my first instructor, and over time, a long-time friend and mentor.

Over the years, I've used a range of machines, including the Facetron, Ultra-Tec V5, Ultra-Tec Fantasy, and my current machine, the Facette Gem Master II. Along the way, I've made countless friends and discoveries. And 20+ years later, I'm still learning.

The desire to write and compile this book came from my need for a faceter-focused resource that brought together basic and advanced information in one place. I wanted a tool where gem cutters could take notes, track rough and cut stones, and even diagram and plot a gem as it's being worked. This book isn't meant to teach faceting from scratch, there are already great books for that. Instead, I hope it becomes a practical, well-used companion whether you're cutting at the bench, identifying stones in the field, or managing your gem business.

When our first print run is gone, I plan to update and expand it for a second edition. Don't hesitate to reach out if you have ideas or features you'd like to see included. I'm pretty easy to find!

Dan Lynch, Gem Cutter, GIA GG

Gemstone Diagrams

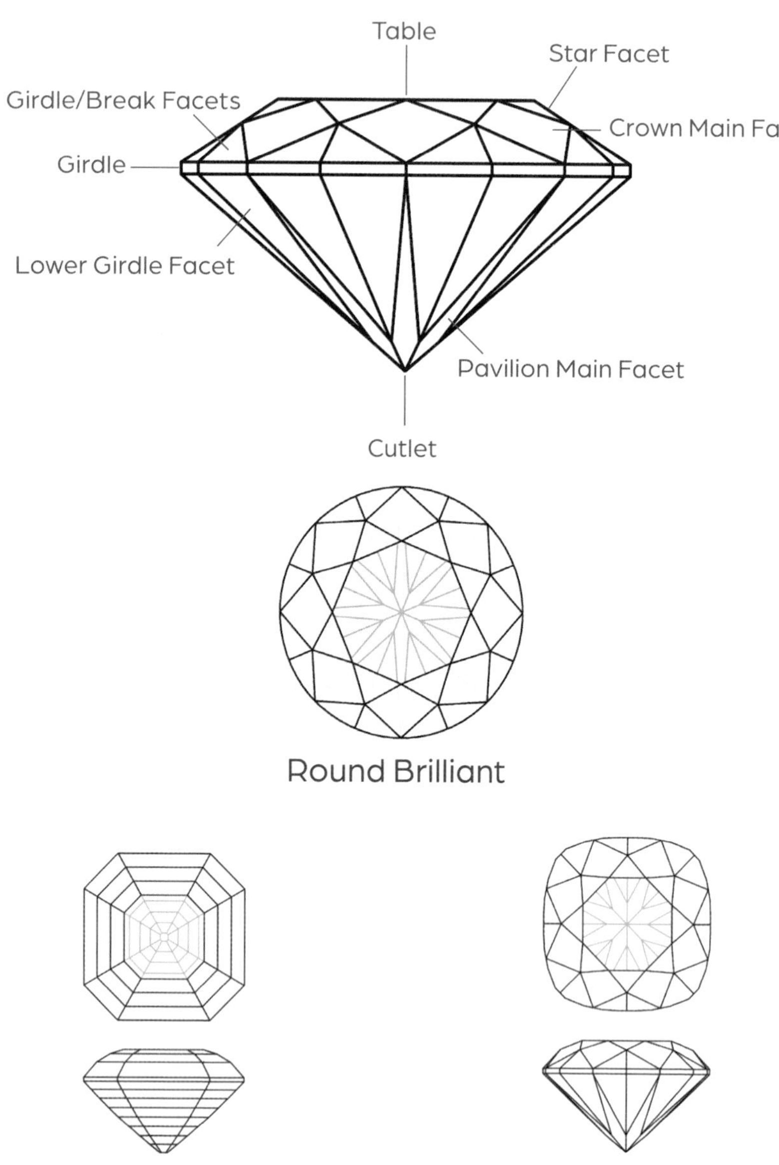

Gemstone Diagrams

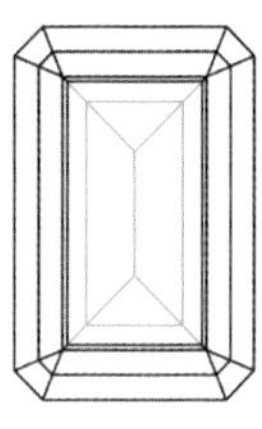
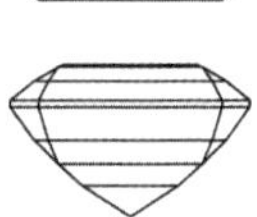

Emerald

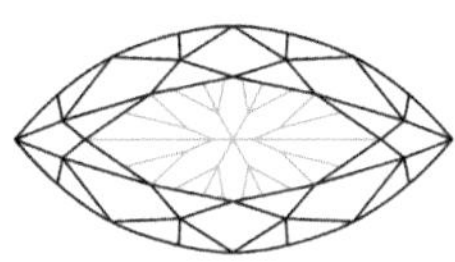
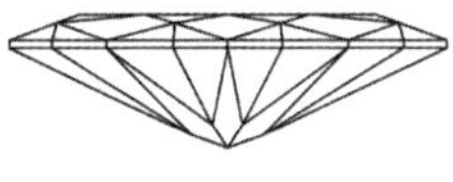

Marquise

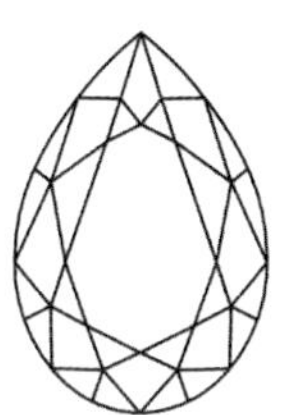
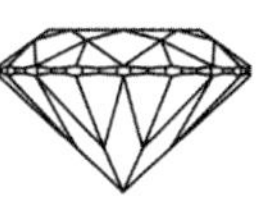

Pear

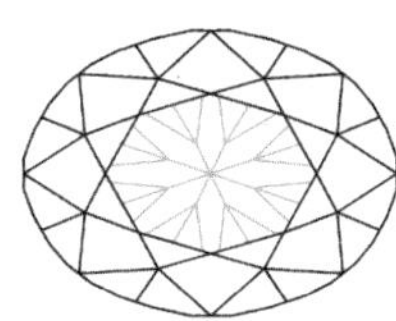
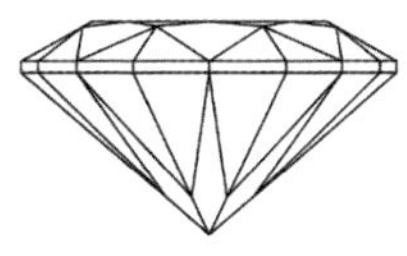

Oval

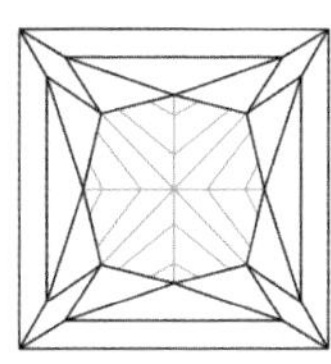
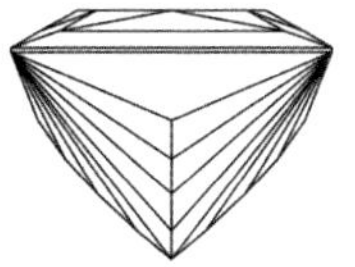

Princess

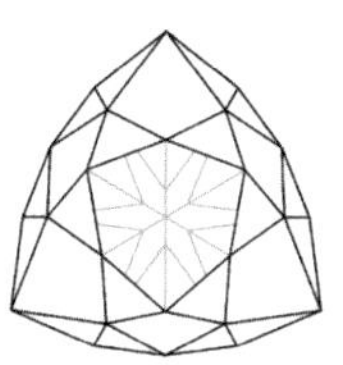
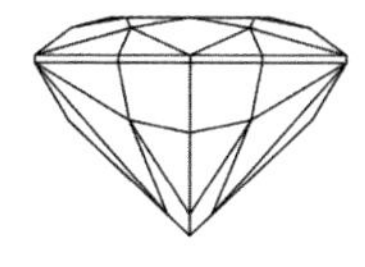

Trillion

Understanding Gemstone Clarity Types

In gemology, gemstones are classified into Type I, Type II, or Type III categories based on their typical level of natural inclusions. This system helps jewelers, gem cutters, and collectors set realistic clarity expectations depending on the species.

Not all gems are judged the same way. Some stones are expected to be flawless, while others naturally contain internal features that do not significantly reduce their beauty or value.

Left: James St John (CC-BY SA 2.0), Mid: Robert M. Lavinsky (CC-BY SA 3.0), Right: Cacoush (CC-BY SA 4.0).

Type I Gemstones: Naturally Eye-Clean

Definition:

Type I gemstones are generally found without visible inclusions. Inclusions are rare and, if present, are minor and difficult to detect without magnification. Buyers expect high clarity in these stones.

Common Type I Gemstones:

- Aquamarine
- Topaz
- Zircon
- Tanzanite
- Amethyst and other Quartz varieties

Faceting Tip:

Type I stones should be carefully evaluated for internal perfection. Even small inclusions can affect marketability.

Aquamarine photo © Peter Torraca

Type II Gemstones: Minor Inclusions Expected

Definition:

Type II gemstones typically have some inclusions.
Clean examples are valuable, but slight inclusions are common and acceptable as long as they do not seriously affect transparency or durability.

Common Type II Gemstones:

- Ruby (Corundum)
- Sapphire (Corundum)
- Spinel
- Garnet species (like Rhodolite, Malaya)
- Iolite
- Alexandrite (Chrysoberyl)
- Tourmaline green/blue

Faceting Tip:

Focus on enhancing color and brilliance, and work around inclusions when possible. Minor inclusions do not significantly diminished desirability.

Tourmaline photo © Roger Dery

Type III Gemstones: Inclusions Are Normal

Definition:

Type III gemstones are almost always included, even in the finest quality stones. Visible inclusions are expected and do not severely reduce the stone's beauty or value when color and transparency are strong.

Common Type III Gemstones:

- Emerald
- Red Beryl
- Tourmaline (especiallyRubelite and Paraíba varieties)
- Kyanite

Faceting Tip:

Prioritize color, vibrancy, and overall transparency. Accept inclusions as part of the gem's natural character. Protective settings may help safeguard more fragile gems.

Emerald photo © Dan Lynch

What's Acceptable and What to Watch For

Many gemstones on the market today are treated to enhance their color, clarity, or durability. While treatments can make gems more beautiful and affordable, disclosure is essential to maintain trust and transparency in the jewelry trade.

Treatments are generally divided into standard accepted practices and treatments requiring disclosure. See legal requirements below.

Common and Generally Accepted Treatments

These treatments are widely practiced, considered normal in the industry, and usually do not require special warnings, though full disclosure is still ethically encouraged:

1. Heat Treatment

- Used on: Ruby, sapphire, aquamarine, zircon, topaz, tourmaline.
- Purpose: Improve color and clarity.

Notes: Stable and permanent under normal wear.

2. Irradiation (Often Followed by Heating)

- Used on: Blue topaz, some colored diamonds.
- Purpose: Alter or intensify color.

Notes: Typically stable; should be disclosed.

3. Oil and Resin Infusion

- Used on: Emeralds and red beryl.
- Purpose: Improve clarity by filling surface-reaching fractures.

Notes: Common practice, but the type of filler (natural oil vs. polymer resin) must be disclosed if known.

4. Surface Coating

- Used on: Quartz (e.g., "mystic topaz" effect), topaz, pearls.
- Purpose: Add iridescence or change surface color.
- Coating can be removed by polishing

Notes: Coatings can wear off; disclosure required.

Treatments Requiring Full Disclosure

The following treatments must be disclosed because they significantly alter the gem, affect durability, or are not considered standard:

1. Fracture Filling (with Glass, Resins, or Polymers)

- Used on: Ruby, sapphire, aquamarine, diamond.

Notes: Filled stones may appear beautiful but are more fragile; heat, ultrasonic cleaning, or solvents can damage the filling material.

2. Diffusion Treatment

- Used on: Sapphire, sometimes spinel.

Notes: Color is introduced on the surface of the gem and at times throughout the gem. Scratches or recutting can reveal different interior color—full disclosure required.

3. Dyeing

- Used on: Turquoise, lapis lazuli, pearls, jade.

Notes: Dye may fade or bleed over time. It must always be disclosed.

4. Laser Drilling

- Used on: Diamond.

Notes: Laser holes made to bleach or remove inclusions. Enhances apparent clarity but creates permanent structural features.

5. Synthetic Overgrowth

- Used on: Corundum, spinel.

  Notes: A synthetic layer is grown over a natural core. The gem is no longer considered fully "natural." Requires clear disclosure.

Legal and Ethical Requirements

U.S. Federal Trade Commission (FTC) Guidelines:

- Sellers must disclose any treatment if it affects the gem's value, stability, or requires special care.
- Misrepresenting a treated gem as "natural" or "untreated" is illegal and considered fraud.

Industry Best Practices:

- Always disclose treatments clearly at the point of sale, in written descriptions when possible.
- When in doubt, assume disclosure is needed.

Cutter's Watchlist

- Ask if a gem has been treated, especially for emeralds, sapphires, rubies, and topaz.
- Get any treatment disclosures in writing for valuable purchases.
- Be cautious with heavily treated gems in jewelry that undergoes repair work (e.g., heating can damage fracture-filled stones).
- Understand that untreated gems often command a premium, but many treated gems offer excellent beauty and value when properly disclosed.

Quick Reference

Treatment	Examples	Disclosure?	Notes
Heat	Ruby, sapphire, aquamarine	Optional (good practice)	Permanent
Irradiation	Blue topaz, colored diamonds	Recommended	Stable
Oil/Resin Infusion	Emerald	Required	May need maintenance
Fracture Filling	Ruby, diamond	Required	Reduces durability
Surface Coating	Quartz, topaz, pearls	Required	Coatings may wear
Dyeing	Turquoise, pearls, jade	Required	Color can fade
Diffusion	Sapphire	Required	Surface-only color

Tips for the Faceter

Older gemstones often show signs of wear, surface scratches, abrasions, minor chips, or dulled facets. With skill, a faceter can restore brilliance, structure, and value to these worn gems. However, gemstone repair requires special care, patience, practice, and judgment.

Assess Before You Cut

Examine Damage Thoroughly

- Use magnification to inspect for scratches, facet abrasions, girdle chips, fractures, or cleavage planes.
- Identify whether damage is superficial or structural (especially important for brittle stones like emerald or zircon).

Know the Gemstone's Properties

- Understand cleavage planes, fracture tendencies, and heat sensitivity.
- Fragile stones like tanzanite, kyanite, topaz, and feldspars require extra caution.

Decide if Recutting, Repolishing, or Simple Touch-Up is Appropriate

- Minor surface wear may only require re-polishing facets.
- Deeper chips or broken facets often require full re-faceting to maintain symmetry and proportions.

Tips for Successful Repairs

1. Minimal Removal First

- Start by lightly polishing worn facets before deciding to re-cut deeply.
- Always preserve as much weight as possible.

2. Protect Fragile Gems

- Use softer laps for brittle stones.
- Avoid excessive heat buildup during polishing to prevent thermal shock, especially in gems like tourmaline, tanzanite, and opal.

3. Re-Establish Critical Facets

- Reset the table and crown mains if necessary; uneven repair can make worn damage more obvious rather than less.
- Girdle integrity is essential: chipped girdles should be rounded and polished to prevent further breakage.

4. Reset Indexes Carefully

- When reworking old stones, align to the original facet pattern if possible to minimize material loss.
- For badly worn stones, consider new cutting plans adapted to the remaining shape.

Cautions and Risks

Heat Sensitivity:

- Avoid aggressive polishing speeds or pressure with stones sensitive to heat (tanzanite, peridot, opal, treated stones).

Treatment Considerations:

- Stones that have been fracture-filled (emeralds, rubies) can be damaged or destroyed during repolishing.
- Assume emeralds and heavily included stones may be oiled or treated unless confirmed otherwise.

Thin Stones:

- Older stones may already be shallow from previous repairs. Be cautious of over-thinning tables or crowns.

When Not to Attempt Repair

- Extensive fractures that compromise the gem's structural integrity.
- Treated gems (fracture-filled, heavily oiled) where reworking will cause visible damage.
- Extremely soft or heat-sensitive gems require specialized equipment and experience.

In these cases, offering a replacement stone or advising resetting with protective designs is often better than risking additional loss.

Mohs Hardness Scale

The Mohs Hardness Scale, developed by Friedrich Mohs in 1812, is a relative scale ranking minerals by their resistance to scratching. It ranges from 1 (very soft) to 10 (the hardest known natural substance—diamond). Each level indicates a mineral that can scratch those below it.

However, the scale is not linear, and this is critical to understand. For example, while diamond ranks just one level higher than corundum (ruby and sapphire), it is approximately 4 times harder in absolute terms. This dramatic increase in hardness between 9 and 10 is a major reason diamond performs so well in both jewelry and industrial applications.

Mohs Hardness Scale with Common Gemstones

Hardness	Mineral Reference	Examples of Gemstones
10	Diamond	Diamond (~4× harder than corundum)
9	Corundum	Ruby, Sapphire
8.5	Chrysoberyl	Alexandrite, Cubic Zirconia
8	Topaz	Blue Topaz, Imperial Topaz
7.5 – 8	Beryl	Emerald, Aquamarine, Morganite, Heliodor
7	Quartz	Amethyst, Citrine, Ametrine, Rock Crystal, Smoky Quartz
6.5 – 7	Garnet	Almandine, Pyrope, Tsavorite, Spessartine
6 – 6.5	Feldspar	Moonstone, Labradorite, Amazonite, Sunstone
5 – 6	Apatite / Glass	Apatite, Obsidian, Glass, Lapis Lazuli, Opal
4 – 5	Fluorite	Fluorite, Malachite, Rhodochrosite
3 – 4	Calcite	Calcite, Azurite, Chrysocolla
2 – 3	Gypsum	Amber, Jet
1	Talc	(Not used in jewelry)

Birthstone Chart by Month

Month	Modern Birthstone(s)	Traditional / Alternate Stones
January	Garnet (usually red varieties)	Rose Quartz, Onyx
February	Amethyst	Bloodstone
March	Aquamarine, Bloodstone	Jasper, Red Coral
April	Diamond	Rock Crystal (Quartz), White Sapphire
May	Emerald	Chrysoprase, Agate
June	Pearl, Alexandrite, Moonstone	Moonstone, Cat's Eye
July	Ruby	Carnelian, Turquoise
August	Peridot, Spinel	Sardonyx
September	Sapphire	Lapis Lazuli
October	Opal, Tourmaline (commonly pink)	Rose Zircon, Aquamarine
November	Topaz (often yellow), Citrine	Golden Beryl (Heliodor), Pearl
December	Turquoise, Zircon, Tanzanite	Blue Topaz, Lapis Lazuli

Birthstones by Month: Traditional and Modern

The concept of birthstones has existed for centuries, rooted in the biblical Breastplate of Aaron and later shaped by cultural, mystical, and commercial traditions.

Today, birthstones are recognized in both traditional (historic or cultural) and modern (standardized by the jewelry trade) forms. The modern list, formalized by the Jewelers of America and the American Gem Society, is the most widely accepted in commercial jewelry today.

Noteworthy Details

- June, October, November, and December each have multiple modern stones, reflecting expanded options for color and budget.
- Spinel was added in 2016 as an official modern birthstone for August.
- Tanzanite, discovered in 1967, was added in 2002 as a modern December birthstone.

Anniversary Chart

Anniversary	Traditional Gift	Modern / Contemporary Gift
1st	Gold Jewelry	Peridot
2nd	Garnet	Garnet
3rd	Pearl	Crystal or Jade
4th	Blue Topaz	Blue Topaz
5th	Sapphire	Sapphire
6th	Amethyst	Amethyst or Turquoise
7th	Onyx / Yellow Sapphire	Onyx
8th	Tourmaline	Tourmaline or Tanzanite
9th	Lapis Lazuli	Lapis Lazuli
10th	Diamond Jewelry	Diamond Jewelry
11th	Turquoise	Turquoise
12th	Jade	Jade
13th	Citrine	Citrine
14th	Opal	Opal
15th	Ruby	Ruby
20th	Emerald	Emerald
25th	Silver (Jubilee)	Tsavorite (Green Garnet) / Silver
30th	Pearl	Pearl
35th	Emerald	Emerald or Jade
40th	Ruby	Ruby
45th	Sapphire	Sapphire
50th	Gold (Jubilee)	Golden Topaz / Gold
55th	Alexandrite	Alexandrite
60th	Diamond (Jubilee)	Diamond
65th	Blue Sapphire	Blue Sapphire
70th	Platinum	Platinum
75th	Diamond	Diamond

The Dopping Process: Attaching the Gemstone

Before a faceter can begin cutting, the gemstone must be securely attached to a "dop stick," a metal rod, typically made of brass or aluminum, designed to fit precisely into the quill of the faceting machine. This process is known as *dopping*, and it's one of the most crucial early steps in ensuring accuracy, stability, and safety during faceting.

There are two primary methods of doping: wax doping and adhesive (glue) doping.

Wax doping is the traditional approach. It involves heating a special dop wax until it becomes pliable, then using it to bond the gem to the dop. The stone is usually warmed slightly to promote adhesion. Once aligned and cooled, the wax hardens to form a solid bond. This method is favored for its speed, reversibility, and cost-effectiveness.

Pros of wax dopping:

- Used by most professional gem cutters
- Quick to apply and remove
- Reheatable and reusable
- Economical
- Allows repositioning when wax is warm

Cons of wax dopping:

- Sensitive to heat (can loosen during polishing)
- Less secure for small or heat-sensitive stones
- Requires a steady hand and experience to align properly

Glue dopping, on the other hand, uses modern adhesives such as epoxy or cyanoacrylate (super glue) to secure the stone. This method is becoming increasingly popular due to its strong bond and suitability for delicate materials.

Pros of glue dopping:

- Strong, reliable bond—especially for small or fragile stones
- No heat required (ideal for heat-sensitive gems)
- Reduces movement during polishing and fine cutting
- Easier for beginners

Cons of glue dopping:

- Longer cure time (unless using quick-setting adhesives)
- Harder to reposition once set
- Requires solvents or mechanical methods for removal
- CA glue is weakened by water, and stones can come off the dop during faceting

Ultimately, the choice between wax and glue hinges on the stone, the cutter's preference, and the nature of the work being done. Many experienced faceters use both methods interchangeably or even employ a hybrid approach that combines wax and glue, tailored to the specific needs of the project.

Photo © Roger Dery

Types of Dop Wax for Gem Faceting

The choice of dop wax plays a critical role in securing the gemstone during the faceting process. Each type of wax offers a different balance of strength, pliability, and temperature sensitivity. Below are the most commonly used dop waxes, listed by hardness and melting temperature.

Type	Melting Temperature	Best For	Properties
Black Dop Wax (Standard Hard)	~165–175°F (74–80°C)	Most gem materials under typical faceting conditions	Provides the strongest bond; excellent for maintaining precise angles; becomes brittle when cold, making removal easier but requiring care during dopping
Green Dop Wax (Medium Hard)	~150–160°F (66–71°C)	General-purpose use on medium to hard stones	Slightly softer than black wax; easier to shape and remove while still offering a secure hold
Red Dop Wax (Soft-Medium)	~130–140°F (54–60°C)	Softer or heat-sensitive gems such as fluorite or opal	Lower melting point reduces risk of thermal shock; easier to remove but may not hold up under extended polishing sessions
Brown Dop Wax (Soft/Flexible)	~120–130°F (49–54°C)	Small, fragile, or highly heat-sensitive stones	Very tacky and pliable when warm; ideal for beginners or stones prone to cracking under thermal stress; not recommended for heavy cutting or high friction polishing

Selection Tips

- Black Wax is used by Professional faceters for its strong hold and stability during all stages of cutting and polishing.
- Green wax offers a good balance for those wanting strength with a little more workability. Often used when cabbing.
- Red wax is favored when working with stones prone to heat or pressure damage.
- Brown wax excels in applications requiring flexibility and gentle adhesion, such as small or delicate stones.

Choosing the right wax for your project ensures that the stone stays secure while allowing for clean removal and minimal risk of damage. Many experienced faceters keep a range of wax types on hand and match the wax to the stone's physical and thermal properties.

Heat Treatment

Heat treatment is one of the oldest and most common enhancements used to improve the color, clarity, and overall appearance of gemstones. By carefully controlling the heating process, certain chemical and structural changes can be induced in the crystal lattice of the stone, resulting in more desirable optical properties.

Commonly Heat-Treated Gemstones

Gemstone	Purpose of Heating	Typical Temp Range	Duration
Sapphire	Intensify or alter color, improve clarity	1600–1900°C (2900–3450°F)	Several hours to several days
Ruby	Remove silk (rutile), enhance red color	1700–1800°C (3100–3300°F)	12–30 hours
Aquamarine	Remove greenish tint, intensify blue	400–500°C (750–930°F)	2–8 hours
Zircon	Change brown or reddish tones to blue	900–1000°C (1650–1830°F) Oxygen reduced envir.	1–2 hours (or longer)
Topaz (rare)	Stabilize or lighten certain tones	~450°C (840°F)	Several hours
Tanzanite	Change brownish material to violet-blue	500–600°C (930–1100°F)	30 minutes to a few hours
Tourmaline	Improve color saturation or lighten dark tones	600–750°C (1100–1380°F)	1–6 hours
Amethyst Citrine	Turn purple quartz into yellow/orange citrine	450–550°C (840–1020°F)	1–3 hours
Ametrine	Create bicolor amethyst-citrine zones	480–550°C (900–1020°F)	Precise control; duration varies

Note: These temperatures are approximate and depend on gem origin, chemistry, and intended result. Exceeding safe thresholds may cause cracking, clouding, or undesired color shifts.

Cautions and Considerations

- Not all stones respond predictably to heat, test on lower-value material first.
- Inclusions, internal strain, or previous treatments can cause stones to crack or fracture.
- Always allow for gradual heating and cooling to avoid thermal shock.
- Tourmaline – note that closed c-axis tourmaline is generally not heat treatable

While most heat treatment occurs in high-temperature kilns, some gemstones, particularly zircons from East Africa, can be effectively treated using simpler tools. These zircons often appear dark brown or nearly black in their rough state but can be transformed into vibrant hues of orange, red, yellow, or pink through heating.

Zircons and Flame Heating

East African zircons, particularly those from Tanzania and Madagascar, are often treated using open flame techniques. These stones generally require temperatures between 800–1000°C (1470–1830°F), which can be achieved with an alcohol lamp, propane torch, or even a stove-top burner.

Faceters who work with these zircons often place the stones in a small crucible or metal dish filled with sand or borax to buffer the heat and reduce the risk of thermal shock. The color change can occur within minutes to an hour, depending on the temperature and the initial chemistry of the stone.

This makes zircon one of the few gemstones that can be successfully and safely heat-treated without expensive equipment, making it a favorite among hobbyist lapidaries experimenting with enhancement.

Natural Gem Species

Agate

RI	1.530–1.540	**Critical Angle**	41.5°
Birefringence	0.004	**Cleavage**	None
SG	2.60–2.64	**Heat sensitivity**	Low
Color	Varies	**Polish methods**	Cerium oxide
Spectrum	Featureless	**Hardness**	6.5–7

Agate is a well-known variety of cryptocrystalline quartz that forms in concentric layers within volcanic rock cavities. Its name dates back to ancient Sicily, and its use as a gemstone spans cultures and centuries. Agate is primarily composed of chalcedony, a microcrystalline form of quartz, and is celebrated for its banding, translucence, and variety of colors and inclusions.

Agates form over long periods as silica-rich groundwater deposits successive layers into hollow cavities, creating distinctive patterns. Their appearance ranges from striking banded formations to picture-like scenes, often enhanced by cutting and polishing. Agate has long been used for jewelry, carvings, cameos, seals, and ornamental items.

Among its many varieties, Moss Agate stands out for its ethereal and organic inclusions. Rather than traditional banding, Moss Agate features fern-like or mossy inclusions of manganese or iron oxides suspended in a translucent chalcedony base, which is often colorless, white, or faintly green. Despite its name, Moss Agate contains no actual plant matter. These inclusions create delicate, branching patterns that evoke natural landscapes, giving each stone a one-of-a-kind appearance.

Moss Agate has no cleavage and takes a good polish, making it suitable for cabochons and freeform shapes. With a hardness of about 6.5–7 on the Mohs scale, it is durable enough for most jewelry applications. It is commonly sourced from India, the United States (Montana, Oregon), Brazil, and Indonesia.

Moss Agate remains a favorite among collectors and artisans alike.

Andalusite

RI	1.629–1.650	**Critical Angle**	37.6°
Birefringence	0.010–0.013	**Cleavage**	Distinct in one direction
SG	3.1–3.2	**Heat sensitivity**	Moderately
Color	Green, yellow, brown, reddish	**Polish methods**	Aluminum Oxide and Diamond
Spectrum	Weak bands at 610, 580, 520 nm	**Hardness**	7.5

Andalusite is an aluminum silicate mineral prized for its striking pleochroism—the ability to display different colors when viewed from various angles. Depending on orientation, a single andalusite gemstone can show shades of green, red, and brown all at once. The stone's name originates from Andalusia, a region in Spain where it was first described, though it occurs in various metamorphic rocks worldwide.

Geologically, andalusite's strongest characteristic is its strong trichroism. It crystallizes in the orthorhombic system and is typically cut to enhance its color zoning, creating a mosaic of earth-toned hues within a single stone. This optical complexity makes it a favorite among gem cutters seeking both a challenge and a dynamic result.

Andalusite has a relatively compact structure and is durable enough for most jewelry applications. However, its visual appeal lies more in its natural beauty than in its brilliance. It is not typically treated, and its unusual color combinations can make it challenging to substitute or imitate.

Historically underappreciated, andalusite has gained popularity with collectors and artisans for its earthy palette and optical intrigue. Its distinctive character sets it apart in a gem world often focused on brilliance alone. High-quality rough can be difficult to obtain, so if you run across it, grab it while you can!

Apatite

RI	1.632–1.654	**Critical Angle**	37.7°
Birefringence	0.002–0.008	**Cleavage**	Poor in one direction
SG	3.1–3.2	**Heat sensitivity**	Yes
Color	Green, blue, yellow, violet, colorless	**Polish methods**	Cerium oxide
Spectrum	Lines near 580, 620 nm	**Hardness**	5

Apatite is a group of phosphate minerals best known for their vibrant range of colors and glassy luster. Its name comes from the Greek apatein, meaning "to deceive," because it was often mistaken for other gems such as beryl or peridot. While primarily a mineral found in sedimentary and igneous environments, gem-quality apatite is valued for its striking appearance and unusual optical properties.

Geologically, apatite occurs in shades of neon blue, green, yellow, violet, and colorless varieties, with the vivid "Paraiba-like" blue green being especially prized. It crystallizes in the hexagonal system and exhibits strong pleochroism, sometimes showing different colors from different angles. Though it can be faceted into dazzling gems, it is relatively soft and brittle, requiring care during cutting and wearing. It is also highly heat sensitive, so it will fracture easily if exposed to too much heat during the doping process.

Apatite is also noteworthy for its double refraction, which can cause some stones to look slightly "fuzzy." Despite its fragility, its affordability and intense colors have earned it a following among collectors and gem artists.

Due to its gemological quirks and bold color palette, apatite offers a rewarding challenge for faceters and an eye-catching result for those drawn to less conventional stones.

Photo: Texas Lane (CC BY-SA 4.0)

Axinite

RI	1.675 – 1.704	**Critical Angle**	36.1°
Birefringence	0.010 – 0.018	**Cleavage**	Distinct in one direction
SG	3.2 – 3.3	**Heat sensitivity**	Moderately
Color	Brown, violet, blue, green	**Polish methods**	Aluminum Oxide
Spectrum	Broad absorption, sometimes near 500–600 nm	**Hardness**	6.5–7

Axinite is a group of calcium aluminum borosilicate minerals known for their distinctive blade-like crystal shape and rich, earthy colors. The name derives from the Greek axine, meaning "axe," referring to the sharp angles of its natural crystals. The most common variety, ferro-axinite, owes its deep brown to purplish tones to its iron content.

Geologically, axinite is appreciated for its pleochroism, typically showing shades of brown, violet, and even blue depending on viewing angle. It crystallizes in the triclinic system and, when faceted, offers a unique visual effect with subtle internal color shifts. The mineral also has strong birefringence, which can contribute to a slightly doubled facet appearance.

Axinite can be brittle and prone to chipping during cutting. Its color palette and optical complexity make it a rewarding material for experienced faceters, and its rarity ensures continued interest from connoisseurs.

Though not widely known to the general public, axinite holds an esteemed place among collectors and gem cutters for its blend of technical challenge and unusual beauty. Facetable rough is rare.

Rough gem © Roger Dery

Benitoite

RI	1.756–1.804	**Critical Angle**	34.2°
Birefringence	0.048	**Cleavage**	Fine lines at 653 and 620 nm
SG	3.6–3.7	**Heat sensitivity**	No
Color	Blue, violetish-blue	**Polish methods**	Aluminum Oxide and Diamond
Spectrum	Featureless	**Hardness**	6.5

Benitoite is a rare blue barium titanium silicate gemstone, famous for its striking sapphire-like color and high dispersion. It was first discovered in 1907 near the San Benito River in California, from which its name is derived. Benitoite is notable for crystallizing in the hexagonal system and often forming perfect triangular-shaped crystals.

The gem's optical properties are remarkable: intense fire, high brilliance, and distinct pleochroism, shifting between blue and near colorless depending on viewing angle. Faceted benitoite, when properly cut, exhibits a lively play of light and a vivid royal to sky-blue hue.

Due to its rarity and gemological uniqueness, benitoite has earned recognition among collectors and connoisseurs. It is also the official state gem of California. Though delicate compared to more common gemstones, benitoite's beauty and scarcity have secured its place as one of the most coveted American gemstones.

Photos © Wayne Schrimp

Beryl

RI	1.564–1.600	**Critical Angle**	39.3°
Birefringence	0.005–0.009	**Cleavage**	Indistinct basal
SG	2.6–2.9	**Heat sensitivity**	No
Color	Green, blue, yellow, pink, colorless	**Polish methods**	Aluminum Oxide, Cerium Oxide, and Diamond
Spectrum	Weak lines near 670 nm (green varieties)	**Hardness**	7.5–8

Beryl is one of the cornerstone mineral species of the gem world and loved by gem cutters, famous for producing many beloved varieties such as emerald, aquamarine, morganite, and heliodor. Its name traces back to the ancient Greek word beryllos, once used to describe any greenish-blue stone.

Chemically, a beryllium aluminum silicate, beryl forms in hexagonal prismatic crystals, often large and transparent. Its coloration is influenced by trace elements: chromium and vanadium yield emerald, green; iron produces aquamarine blue; manganese gives morganite its pink tones.

Beryl is prized for its clarity, durability, and versatility in cutting. The crystal structure often allows for large, eye-clean gems, while its relatively high hardness makes it suitable for daily wear. Pleochroism is present in many varieties, subtly affecting color saturation depending on orientation.

For millennia, beryl has been revered for its beauty and perceived metaphysical properties, often associated with protection, healing, and vision. It remains one of the most essential and beloved gem species worldwide.

Photo © Peter Torraca

Major Varieties of Beryl

Emerald

- Color: Rich green to bluish green.
- Trace Elements: Chromium and/or vanadium.
- Key Features: Almost always included ("jardin" effect is typical). High-quality stones are rare and highly valuable.
- Notes: Most emeralds are treated with oil or resin to improve clarity.

Aquamarine

- Color: Pale blue to deep blue green, resembling the sea.
- Trace Elements: Iron.
- Key Features: Typically very clean and transparent; inclusions are rare.
- Notes: Often heat-treated to remove greenish tones and enhance blue.

Morganite

- Color: Soft pink to peach to salmon.
- Trace Elements: Manganese.
- Key Features: Light pastel tones are common; deeper pinks are more valuable.
- Notes: Some stones are heat-treated to improve pink intensity.

Heliodor (Golden Beryl)

- Color: Yellow to golden green.
- Trace Elements: Iron (in a different oxidation state than aquamarine).
- Key Features: Bright, sunny colors; excellent brilliance when well-cut.
- Notes: Less common in the jewelry market compared to aquamarine and emerald.

Emerald, Aquamarine, and Heliodor © Dan Lynch. Morganite: © Peter Torraca,

Goshenite

- Color: Colorless.
- Trace Elements: None (pure beryl).
- Key Features: High transparency and brilliance; historically used as an imitation diamond.
- Notes: May be coated or treated to imitate colored gems today.

Red Beryl (Bixbite)

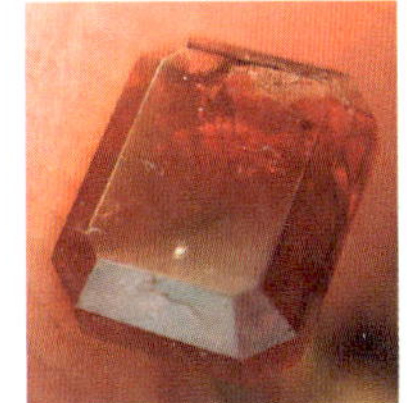

- Color: Intense raspberry red.
- Trace Elements: Manganese.
- Key Features: Extremely rare; found almost exclusively in Utah, USA.
- Notes: Natural crystals are tiny, making facetable stones above 1 carat extraordinarily rare and valuable.

Goshenite © Dan Lynch, Red Beryl © Kell Hymer.

Chrysoberyl

RI	1.746 – 1.755	**Critical Angle**	35°
Birefringence	0.008–0.010	**Cleavage**	Distinct in one direction
SG	3.7–3.8	**Heat sensitivity**	No
Color	Yellow, green, brown, colorless	**Polish methods**	Aluminum Oxide and Diamond
Spectrum	Absorption near 445, 470, 505 nm	**Hardness**	8.5

Chrysoberyl is an aluminum beryllium oxide mineral distinguished by its exceptional hardness, vibrant brilliance, and fascinating optical phenomena. Its name is derived from the Greek words chrysos (gold) and beryllos (a term historically used for blue-green stones), though chrysoberyl is unrelated to true beryl. First recognized as a distinct gem species in the 18th century, it quickly earned admiration for its striking qualities.

Typically found in shades of yellow green to golden-brown, chrysoberyl displays strong pleochroism, showing different colors when viewed from varying angles. Its crystal structure, belonging to the orthorhombic system, contributes to its resilience and brilliance. Two remarkable varieties of chrysoberyl are particularly celebrated: cats-eye chrysoberyl, which displays a sharp, silky line of light across its surface due to needle-like inclusions, and alexandrite, famous for its dramatic color change from green to red under different lighting conditions.

Unenhanced and highly durable, chrysoberyl has been historically prized for its symbolic associations with protection, prosperity, and insight. In gem cutting, it offers both practical hardness and optical fascination, making it a favorite for fine jewelry and high-end collections. Whether admired for its elegant hues or its optical marvels, chrysoberyl is one of the most captivating and versatile gemstones in the mineral world.

Photo © Peter Toccara

Major Varieties of Chrysoberyl

Chrysoberyl (Golden to Greenish Yellow)

- Color: Yellow, greenish-yellow, or brownish tones.
- Trace Elements: Iron influences the greenish coloration.
- Key Features: Strong brilliance and high luster when well-cut; often eye-clean.
- Notes: Often faceted into traditional shapes; durable and suitable for all types of jewelry.

Cat's Eye Chrysoberyl (Cymophane)

- Color: Honey yellow to greenish or brownish shades.
- Trace Elements: Iron.
- Key Features: Exhibits a sharp, luminous cat's eye effect (chatoyancy) when cut en cabochon and caused by parallel inclusions of rutile fibers.
- Notes: The finest cat's eyes display a strong, centered "eye" and a sharp division of light and dark (known as the "milk and honey" effect).

Alexandrite (Color-Change Chrysoberyl)

- Color: Green to bluish green in daylight; red to purplish red under incandescent light.
- Trace Elements: Chromium (similar to emerald).
- Key Features: Dramatic color change is the hallmark of high-quality alexandrite. It shows vivid color in both lighting conditions and a strong, distinct shift.
- Notes:
  - One of the rarest and most valuable gemstones.
  - First discovered in the Ural Mountains of Russia in the 1830s and named after the future Czar Alexander II.
  - Also found today in Brazil, Sri Lanka, India, and East Africa, though the finest Russian stones remain legendary.
  - Synthetic alexandrite is created via Czochralski and floating zone methods for jewelry use.

Clinozoisite

RI	1.725–1.768	**Critical Angle**	36°
Birefringence	0.036–0.048	**Cleavage**	Perfect
SG	3.3 – 3.5	**Heat sensitivity**	Yes
Color	Green, yellow-green, brown	**Polish methods**	Cerium Oxide
Spectrum	Bands at 438, 453, 470, 491 nm	**Hardness**	6–7

Clinozoisite is a calcium aluminum silicate mineral and a prominent member of the epidote group. First described in the mid-19th century, its name reflects its structural relation to zoisite and the inclined angles of its crystal forms ("clino" meaning inclined). Found in metamorphic environments, clinozoisite forms during the regional metamorphism of calcium-rich rocks.

Gem-quality clinozoisite ranges from light green and yellowish green to brownish shades, often with subtle pleochroism visible under polarized light. Crystallizing in the monoclinic system, clinozoisite can produce transparent crystals that, when faceted, display a lively luster and understated brilliance. Although not especially well-known to the general public, it holds significant value among collectors for its clarity and natural, earthy color palette.

Clinozoisite is moderately durable but can be challenging to facet due to its perfect cleavage and internal strain. Skilled cutters orient stones carefully to maximize color and minimize fracture risk. Its quiet beauty and mineralogical importance make it a rewarding specimen for those interested in exploring beyond the traditional boundaries of the gemstone world. As a bridge between more famous minerals like zoisite and epidote, clinozoisite offers a glimpse into the intricate complexity of silicate gem species.

Photo: public domain

Confetti Sunstone

RI	1.537–1.547	**Critical Angle**	41.3°
Birefringence	.007–.010	**Cleavage**	Perfect in two directions
SG	2.65–2.70	**Heat sensitivity**	Moderate
Color	clear, red, orange, yellow, brown, green with multicolored inclusions	**Polish methods**	Cerium Oxide
Spectrum	Featureless	**Hardness**	6–6.5

Confetti Sunstone is a vivid and whimsical variety of feldspar characterized by a dazzling mix of multicolored metallic inclusions, which appear scattered throughout the gem like festive confetti. These inclusions typically consist of copper, hematite, or goethite, creating a sparkling, flashy appearance as the stone moves in the light.

While it is closely related to Oregon Sunstone in chemical composition and mineral group (plagioclase feldspar), Confetti Sunstone tends to exhibit a denser concentration of small inclusions that produce a vibrant, textured effect rather than a smooth schiller. Its base colors often vary from pink to reddish-orange, and the confetti effect incorporates glints of gold, green, silver, and even blue, depending on the orientation and lighting.

Confetti Sunstone is most often associated with sources from India and Tanzania, although some U.S. material also displays this phenomenon. While it may not have the same market prestige as Oregon Sunstone, it is increasingly valued for its visual uniqueness and lively character. The gem is typically cut in cabochon or freeform styles to highlight its internal fireworks.

With a Mohs hardness of approximately 6–6.5, Confetti Sunstone necessitates gentle handling in jewelry but is valued by designers and collectors for its unique appeal and playful natural brilliance.

Photo: © Kell Hymer

Corundum

RI	1.762–1.770	**Critical Angle**	34.4°
Birefringence	0.008	**Cleavage**	None
SG	3.9–4.1	**Heat sensitivity**	No
Color	Colorless, blue, red, pink, yellow, green	**Polish methods**	Diamond
Spectrum	Fine lines at 450, 470, 660, 700 nm	**Hardness**	9

Corundum is one of the most celebrated minerals in the gem world, forming the basis for ruby and sapphire. Composed of aluminum oxide (Al_2O_3), corundum is prized for its extraordinary hardness, second only to diamond, and its wide range of vivid colors. The name stems from the Sanskrit kuruvinda, meaning "ruby," reflecting its ancient recognition.

Trace elements determine corundum's color: chromium produces the deep red of ruby, while iron, titanium, and other elements create the broad palette of sapphires, ranging from blue and pink to yellow, green, and even colorless varieties known as "white sapphire." Crystallizing in the trigonal system, corundum's structure promotes excellent durability and brilliance, making it ideal for both faceting and everyday wear.

Throughout history, corundum gems have symbolized nobility, power, and wisdom. Rubies were worn by warriors for protection, while sapphires adorned clergy and royalty as symbols of divine favor. In modern times, their enduring hardness and beauty continue to make them premier choices for engagement rings and fine jewelry.

Gem-quality corundum offers not only breathtaking color but also optical phenomena such as asterism (in star sapphires and star rubies), which is caused by aligned rutile inclusions. Whether celebrated for its fiery glow or celestial sheen, corundum remains one of the most versatile and revered gems known to humankind.

Photo © Tom Schultz.

Major Varieties of Corundum

Ruby

- Color: Red to purplish red, sometimes slightly orangey-red.
- Trace Elements: Chromium.
- Key Features: The chromium gives ruby its color and causes fluorescence under UV light, intensifying its glow.
- Notes:
  - Fine rubies are rare and highly valuable, especially those with vivid "pigeon's blood" red color and minimal inclusions.
  - Most rubies are heat-treated to enhance color and clarity; fracture-filled rubies require full disclosure.

Sapphire

- Color: Blue is the classic color, but sapphires occur in nearly every hue except red.
- Trace Elements: Iron and titanium for blue; iron alone for yellow and green; vanadium for violet; chromium for pink.
- Key Features: Rich blues are the most prized, especially medium to medium-dark vivid blues (e.g., Kashmir and Ceylon sapphires).
- Notes:
  - Fancy sapphires include pink, yellow, green, purple, orange, and colorless (white sapphire).
  - The rarest fancy sapphire is padparadscha sapphire — a delicate blend of pink and orange resembling a sunset.
  - Heat treatment is standard and accepted industry-wide to improve color and clarity.

Ruby © Roger Dery, Sapphire: © Peter Torraca.

Star Ruby and Star Sapphire

- Color: Any ruby or sapphire body color displaying asterism (a star-like optical phenomenon).
- Trace Elements and Inclusions: Rutile needle inclusions aligned within the crystal structure.
- Key Features: Sharp six-rayed stars are highly prized; the best stars are centered and move gracefully across the stone's surface under light.
- Notes:
    - Star stones are cut into cabochon (rounded, polished, not faceted) to display the star effect best.
    - Flame fusion methods also produce synthetic star corundum.
    - Diffusion treatment is often used to create star effect in synthetics

Cuprite

RI	2.849–2.951
Birefringence	None (Isotropic)
SG	6.1
Color	Red, dark red
Spectrum	Broad absorption below 500 nm
Critical Angle	20.3°
Cleavage	None
Heat sensitivity	Moderately
Polish methods	Cerium Oxide
Hardness	3.5–4

Cuprite is a copper oxide mineral prized for its deep, rich red color and brilliant internal glow. Its name derives from the Latin cuprum, meaning "copper," reflecting its high copper content. Cuprite typically forms in the oxidized zones of copper deposits and is occasionally found as well-formed cubic or octahedral crystals.

In rare cases where transparency is sufficient, cuprite can be faceted into stunning gemstones with a vivid crimson hue and intense internal brilliance. However, the mineral is very soft and brittle, making cut stones extremely fragile and best suited for protected display rather than jewelry wear. Cuprite's high luster and intense color saturation make it visually unforgettable when polished.

Historically, cuprite has been mined more for its copper content than its gem potential, but exceptional crystals—particularly from localities such as Namibia have elevated its stature among collectors. The combination of metallic luster, vibrant color, and scarcity in facetable form ensures that cuprite holds a special place among the world's rarest and most captivating collector gemstones.

Photo © Kell Hymer

Danburite

RI	1.627–1.636	**Critical Angle**	37.9°
Birefringence	0.009	**Cleavage**	Poor
SG	3	**Heat sensitivity**	No
Color	Colorless, yellow, pink	**Polish methods**	Cerium Oxide and Diamond
Spectrum	Weak line at 465 nm	**Hardness**	7–7.5

Danburite is a calcium boron silicate mineral celebrated for its exceptional clarity, brilliance, and gentle beauty. Discovered in Danbury, Connecticut, in the early 19th century—hence its name—danburite often forms in elongated prismatic crystals with sharply defined terminations. When expertly faceted, its transparent crystals can rival topaz or diamond in sparkle.

Typically colorless, pale yellow, or faintly pink, danburite crystallizes in the orthorhombic system and exhibits high transparency and excellent light performance. Its refractive index is similar to quartz but its luster, when polished, is glassier and livelier. Because it combines durability and beauty, danburite is well-suited for jewelry, although it remains less well-known to the broader public.

Its clean, unpretentious beauty and brilliant performance make danburite an elegant, understated alternative to more mainstream colorless gems, providing a sophisticated option for those who value rarity as well as radiance.

Diamond

RI	2.417	**Critical Angle**	24.4°
Birefringence	None (Isotropic)	**Cleavage**	Perfect (octahedral)
SG	3.52	**Heat sensitivity**	No
Color	Colorless, yellow, brown, rare blue/pink/green	**Polish methods**	Diamond Paste
Spectrum	Occasional absorption at 415 nm (Cape series)	**Hardness**	10

Diamond is the ultimate symbol of durability, brilliance, and timeless value. Composed entirely of carbon atoms arranged in a perfect cubic lattice, diamond's extraordinary properties have captivated civilizations for millennia. Its name derives from the Greek adamas, meaning "unconquerable" or "invincible," reflecting its unparalleled hardness and status as a symbol of enduring strength.

Formed deep within the Earth's mantle under intense heat and pressure, diamonds are brought to the surface through volcanic pipes known as kimberlites. Their optical properties—high refractive index, strong dispersion, and adamantine luster—give diamonds unparalleled sparkle and fire. Available in a spectrum of colors, from colorless to hues of yellow, pink, blue, and even rare reds, diamonds are prized for both their beauty and rarity.

Historically, diamonds were reserved for royalty and religious leaders, symbolizing divine strength and purity. Today, they remain the quintessential gemstone for engagement rings and fine jewelry worldwide. Whether appreciated for their natural beauty, industrial utility, or symbolic significance, diamonds are the most iconic gemstone of all.

Diopside

RI	1.663–1.701	**Critical Angle**	36.5°
Birefringence	0.038	**Cleavage**	Distinct in two directions
SG	3.2–3.4	**Heat sensitivity**	No
Color	Green, dark green, black	**Polish methods**	Aluminum Oxide
Spectrum	Lines at 504, 630 nm (chromium-rich)	**Hardness**	5.5–6.5

Diopside is a calcium-magnesium silicate mineral belonging to the pyroxene group. It is admired for its lush green hues and strong, earthy appeal. The mineral's name comes from the Greek words dis (meaning "two") and opsis ("vision"), a reference to its optical properties. Diopside typically forms in metamorphic rocks such as skarns and marbles and crystallizes in the monoclinic system.

Gem-quality diopside typically appears in vivid green shades, though it can also be found in white, gray, or brown. The most prized variety, chrome diopside, owes its rich, intense green to traces of chromium. When properly faceted, diopside exhibits a brilliant luster and good transparency; however, due to its perfect cleavage, it requires careful handling.

Although softer than many traditional gemstones, diopside's vivid color and relative affordability have made it increasingly popular for jewelry in recent years, especially as an accessible alternative to emerald. In metaphysical traditions, diopside is believed to promote healing and emotional balance. Whether admired for its verdant hues or its geological significance, diopside offers a refreshing and accessible beauty in the world of colored gemstones.

Faceted © Didier Descouens, CC BY-SA 4.0, Rough: Rob Lavinsky, iRocks.com

Epidote

RI	1.725–1.768	**Critical Angle**	34.9°
Birefringence	0.043	**Cleavage**	Perfect
SG	3.3–3.5	**Heat sensitivity**	Yes
Color	Green, yellow-green, brown	**Polish methods**	Cerium Oxide
Spectrum	Bands at 438, 453, 470, 491 nm	**Hardness**	6–7

The Epidote group encompasses a variety of closely related silicate minerals, unified by a similar crystal structure but varying slightly in chemical composition. The name "epidote" comes from the Greek epidosis, meaning "increase," alluding to the mineral's tendency to form elongated, well-developed crystals. Epidote group minerals are commonly found in metamorphic rocks, especially those formed through regional metamorphism.

Classic epidote typically displays a pistachio-green to yellow-green color, though some group members, such as clinozoisite, appear more brownish or even pinkish in hue. Crystallizing in the monoclinic system, epidote crystals often exhibit a vitreous luster and strong pleochroism. When faceted, gem-quality epidote reveals lively flashes of yellow and green depending on the viewing angle but cutting requires care due to the mineral's perfect cleavage.

Though not a mainstream jewelry stone, epidote's dynamic color play and relative rarity in transparent form make it a prized specimen for collectors. As a gemstone, epidote offers a rich, organic beauty, connecting the cutter and collector alike to the intricate, evolving forces of the Earth.

Faceted Didier Descouens (CC BY-SA 4.0), Rough: Rob Lavinsky, iRocks.com

Feldspar

RI	1.518–1.575	**Critical Angle**	41°
Birefringence	0.007–0.010	**Cleavage**	Perfect in one or two directions
SG	2.60–2.64	**Heat sensitivity**	Some types (orthoclase) are heat sensitive
Color	Colorless, pink, green, orange, gray	**Polish methods**	Cerium Oxide
Spectrum	Lines vary: 460, 580, 650 nm	**Hardness**	6–6.5

The feldspar group is the most abundant mineral family in the Earth's crust, encompassing a wide range of silicate minerals with similar chemical structures. Derived from the German feld (field) and spath (a non-metallic mineral with perfect cleavage), feldspar minerals are foundational to the formation of rocks such as granite, gneiss, and basalt. In gemology, several feldspar varieties are prized, including moonstone, labradorite, sunstone, and orthoclase.

Gem-quality feldspars exhibit a dazzling range of optical phenomena. Moonstone is celebrated for its adularescence—a soft, glowing sheen across the surface—while labradorite is admired for its vibrant play of spectral colors, known as labradorescence. Sunstone displays aventurescence, a glittering effect caused by metallic inclusions. Depending on the variety, feldspars generally crystallize in the monoclinic or triclinic systems.

Though not as hard as quartz, many feldspar gems are durable enough for jewelry with mindful wear. Their vivid optical effects and variety of colors make them popular choices among designers and collectors. Whether glowing like a distant moon or shimmering with inner fire, feldspars offer a rich, magical palette of natural beauty.

Facedted © Dan Lynch, Rough: Rough: Rob Lavinsky, iRocks.com

Fluorite

RI	1.434	**Critical Angle**	44.3°
Birefringence	None (Isotropic)	**Cleavage**	Perfect in four directions
SG	3.0–3.2	**Heat sensitivity**	Yes
Color	Purple, green, yellow, blue, colorless	**Polish methods**	Cerium Oxide
Spectrum	Varies—band around 490 nm common	**Hardness**	4

Fluorite is a calcium fluoride mineral celebrated for its remarkable range of colors, exceptional clarity, and perfect cubic crystal forms. Its name comes from the Latin fluere, meaning "to flow," a reference to its use as a flux in metallurgical processes. Beyond its industrial significance, fluorite has secured a lasting place in the gem world for its beauty and versatility.

Fluorite's colors span the spectrum—blue, green, purple, yellow, pink, and colorless—often within the same specimen, creating spectacular multicolored gems. It crystallizes in the isometric system, typically forming cubic or octahedral crystals with a bright, vitreous luster. Some fluorite specimens exhibit fluorescence under ultraviolet light, adding another layer of visual intrigue.

Due to its softness and perfect cleavage, fluorite is challenging to facet and unsuitable for everyday jewelry, but it remains a beloved collector's gemstone.

Skilled cutters highlight its vibrant colors and internal clarity, often using special techniques to avoid damage. It remains one of the most colorful and dynamic examples of nature's artistic range, offering endless fascination to those who appreciate subtle beauty and vivid hue.

Faceted: TheUltimateGrass (CC 0), Rough: Marie-Lan Taÿ Pamart (CC BY 4.0)

Garnet

RI	1.730–1.890	**Critical Angle**	43.5°
Birefringence	None (Isotropic)	**Cleavage**	None
SG	3.1–4.3	**Heat sensitivity**	No
Color	Red, orange, green, brown, pink	**Polish methods**	Aluminum Oxide, Tin Oxide, and Diamond
Spectrum	Depends on species—e.g., 504, 520 nm in pyrope	**Hardness**	6.5–7.5

Garnets are a broad group of silicate minerals that share a typical crystal structure but vary widely in chemical composition. The name originates from the Latin granatus, meaning "grain" or "seed," referring to the gem's resemblance to pomegranate seeds. Garnets have been prized since ancient Egypt and Rome for their durability and rich, vivid colors.

While red is the most classic hue, garnets are found in virtually every color of the spectrum, including vibrant greens (tsavorite and demantoid), oranges (spessartine), and rare blues. They crystallize in the isometric system, often forming dodecahedral crystals with high brilliance and a vitreous luster. Garnets are singly refractive, resulting in direct, intense coloration without pleochroism.

Historically associated with protection and vitality, garnets have been treasured in talismans and royal adornments for millennia. Today, they remain highly sought after by collectors and jewelers for their beauty, affordability, and variety. Whether sparkling in fiery reds or glowing in lush greens, garnets offer an extraordinary palette of natural artistry.

Garnets are typically divided into two major groups based on composition: Pyralspite (aluminum-based) and Ugrandite (calcium-based). Many garnets form through solid solution between end members, resulting in a rich variety of color and character.

Pyralspite Series (Aluminum Garnets)

Almandine

- Color: Deep red to purplish red
- Traits: Iron-rich, the most common garnet type; high RI and strong absorption spectrum
- Hardness: ~7.0–7.5
- Rarity: Common

Pyrope

- Color: Blood red to wine red
- Traits: Magnesium-rich; historically known as Bohemian garnet; lower RI than almandine
- Hardness: ~7.0
- Rarity: Common

Spessartine (Spessartite)

- Color: Vivid orange to reddish orange
- Traits: Manganese-rich; highly refractive; prized for brilliance and warm tone
- Hardness: ~7.0–7.5
- Rarity: Uncommon to Rare

Malaya Garnet

- Color: Pinkish-orange, peach, or warm brownish pink
- Traits: Mixture of pyrope and spessartine; found mainly in East Africa
- Hardness: ~7.0–7.5
- Rarity: Rare

Rhodolite

- Color: Raspberry red to purplish pink
- Traits: Mixture of pyrope and almandine; typically, lighter and cleaner than almandine
- Hardness: ~7.0–7.5
- Rarity: Uncommon

Almandine: Rob Lavinsky, iRocks.com, Pyrope: Lech Darski, (CC-BY 4.0), Spessartine: Géry Parent (public domain), Malaya Garnet © Peter Torraca, Rhodolite: YippeeD, CC BY-SA 4.0

Ugrandite Series (Calcium Garnets)

Grossular

- Color: Colorless, green, yellow, pink, orange
- Traits: Calcium-aluminum base; very diverse; includes hessonite and tsavorite varieties
- Hardness: ~6.5–7.0
- Rarity: Uncommon (varies by color)

Hessonite (variety of Grossular)

- Color: Cinnamon orange to brown
- Traits: Distinctively low density and roiled appearance; historically sourced from Sri Lanka and India
- Hardness: ~7.0
- Rarity: Common to Uncommon

Tsavorite (variety of Grossular)

- Color: Intense bright green
- Traits: Vanadium/chromium-rich; one of the most valued garnets for brilliance and color
- Hardness: ~7.0
- Rarity: Rare

Andradite

- Color: Yellow green to dark brown and black
- Traits: Calcium-iron garnet; includes demantoid, melanite, and topazolite varieties
- Hardness: ~6.5–7.0
- Rarity: Rare (especially facet-grade forms)

Demantoid (variety of Andradite)

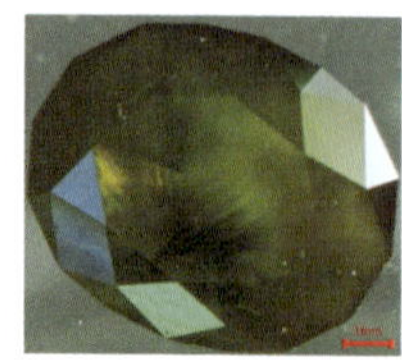

- Color: Bright green to emerald green
- Traits: One of the most brilliant garnets with exceptional dispersion; originally from Russia
- Hardness: ~6.5
- Rarity: Very Rare

Melanite (variety of Andradite)

- Color: Opaque black
- Traits: Often used ornamentally; not typically faceted
- Hardness: ~6.5
- Rarity: Uncommon

Topazolite (variety of Andradite)

- Color: Yellow to golden-brown
- Traits: Rarely seen in jewelry; high luster; brittle
- Hardness: ~6.5
- Rarity: Very Rare

Uvarovite

- Color: Vivid emerald, green (druzy crystals)
- Traits: Chromium-rich; never faceted due to small crystal size; admired in druzy form
- Hardness: ~6.5
- Rarity: Very Rare

Other Garnet Varieties and Hybrids

Color-Change Garnet

- Color: Green to purplish red (in daylight to incandescent light)
- Traits: Rare combination of spessartine and pyrope; alexandrite-like shift
- Hardness: ~7.0
- Rarity: Very Rare

Hydrogrossular

- Color: Light green, grayish-white, pink
- Traits: Typically, opaque or translucent; used more for carving or cabochons than faceting
- Hardness: ~7.0
- Rarity: Uncommon

Idocrase

RI	1.698–1.723	**Critical Angle**	35.6°
Birefringence	0.025	**Cleavage**	Poor
SG	3.3–3.5	**Heat sensitivity**	Moderate
Color	Green, brown, yellow	**Polish methods**	Cerium Oxide and Diamond
Spectrum	Weak lines around 520 nm	**Hardness**	6.5

Idocrase, more commonly known as vesuvianite, is a complex silicate mineral named after Mount Vesuvius, where it was first discovered. The name "idocrase" comes from the Greek eidos (form) and krasis (mixture), referencing its varied crystal habit and composition.

Vesuvianite typically forms in skarns and metamorphosed limestones and can range in color from green to brown, yellow, blue, and even purple. It crystallizes in the tetragonal system and often shows strong pleochroism, especially in richer-colored stones. Transparent specimens can be faceted into gems with a bright, vitreous luster.

Though not as widely known as more mainstream green stones, vesuvianite's durability and bright colors make it an appealing choice for collectors and designers seeking something different. Vesuvianite represents a vibrant and versatile addition to the family of colored gemstones.

Photo © Daniel Stair.

Iolite

RI	1.434	**Critical Angle**	40°
Birefringence	None (Isotropic)	**Cleavage**	Perfect in four directions
SG	3.0–3.2	**Heat sensitivity**	Yes
Color	Purple, green, yellow, blue, colorless	**Polish methods**	Cerium Oxide
Spectrum	Varies—band around 490 nm common	**Hardness**	7–7.5

Iolite, the gem-quality variety of cordierite, is famed for its striking pleochroism—it shows different colors depending on viewing direction, typically deep violet-blue to yellow gray. The name iolite is derived from the Greek ios, meaning "violet," while cordierite honors French geologist Pierre Cordier. Iolite is commonly referred to as water sapphire.

Iolite crystallizes in the orthorhombic system and often occurs in metamorphic rocks. It can produce sizable, transparent crystals that are ideal for faceting. Its strong pleochroism can present both a challenge and a delight for gem cutters, who must orient the stones carefully to maximize the desired color. When properly cut, iolite offers a rich, saturated hue reminiscent of sapphire, but at a more accessible price point.

Historically used by Viking navigators as a polarizing lens to locate the sun on cloudy days, iolite carries a legacy of adventure and exploration. It remains a popular gemstone today, offering vibrant beauty with a touch of historical mystique.

Kornerupine

RI	1.730–1.890	**Critical Angle**	43.5°
Birefringence	None (Isotropic)	**Cleavage**	None
SG	3.1–4.3	**Heat sensitivity**	No
Color	Red, orange, green, brown, pink	**Polish methods**	Aluminum Oxide, Tin Oxide, and Diamond
Spectrum	Depends on species—e.g., 504, 520 nm in pyrope	**Hardness**	6.5–7

Kornerupine is a rare and striking borosilicate mineral prized by collectors and gem cutters for its pleochroism—the ability to display multiple colors depending on the viewing angle. The stone can range from deep green to brown, yellow-green, and even bluish hues, with its most valuable variety being the vibrant emerald-like green to blue green known as "chrome kornerupine," due to its chromium content. First discovered in 1884 in Greenland and named after Danish geologist Andreas Nikolaus Kornerup, the gem has since been found in a few select locations, including Madagascar, Tanzania, Sri Lanka, and Myanmar.

From a gemological perspective, Kornerupine has a hardness of 6.5 to 7 on the Mohs scale, making it suitable for jewelry, though it requires care to prevent scratching. It possesses a refractive index of approximately 1.660–1.703 and a birefringence of 0.036–0.037, which enhance its lively optical performance. Its distinct pleochroism can be intense, particularly in vividly colored stones, making orientation during faceting essential to achieve the desired face-up color.

Despite its rarity, Kornerupine remains relatively unknown in the commercial market, primarily due to its limited availability and modest marketing. However, among connoisseurs, it holds a niche appeal—especially the chrome-rich varieties, which can rival fine tourmaline or tsavorite garnet in beauty. As a result, Kornerupine is regarded as both a collector's gem and a unique, conversation-starting addition to any fine jewelry collection.

Photo © Daniel Stair.

Kyanite

RI	1.710–1.734	**Critical Angle**	35.5°
Birefringence	0.024	**Cleavage**	Perfect in one direction
SG	3.6–3.7	**Heat sensitivity**	Yes
Color	Blue, green, colorless, gray	**Polish methods**	Cerium Oxide
Spectrum	Bands near 450, 470, 525 nm	**Hardness**	4.5–7

Kyanite is an aluminum silicate mineral best known for its deep blue color and pronounced directional hardness—a rare property where hardness varies depending on crystallographic orientation. Its name comes from the Greek kyanos, meaning "blue," though kyanite can also appear green, gray, or colorless.

Crystallizing in the triclinic system, kyanite often forms elongated, blade-like crystals with a vitreous to pearly luster. It can display a luminous, saturated color rivaling sapphire when properly faceted. However, its variable hardness and perfect cleavage make it one of the more challenging gems to cut.

Despite these difficulties, kyanite's intense beauty and unique properties have earned it a niche following. In the hands of a skilled cutter, kyanite reveals a mesmerizing, almost liquid depth of color, offering a vivid glimpse into the mineral world's more complex creations.

Moldavite

RI	1.480–1.510	**Critical Angle**	42°
Birefringence	None (Amorphous)	**Cleavage**	Conchoidal fracture
SG	2.32–2.38	**Heat sensitivity**	Yes
Color	Green, olive green	**Polish methods**	Cerium Oxide
Spectrum	None distinctive	**Hardness**	5.5

Moldavite is a natural green glass formed approximately 15 million years ago during a meteorite impact in what is now the Czech Republic. It is classified as a tektite, a type of impact glass, and its name derives from the Moldau River region (Vltava in Czech) where it was first found.

Moldavite's color ranges from olive green to deep forest green and occasionally brownish green. Its surface frequently displays intricate, etched textures, a result of atmospheric sculpting during its fiery descent. When faceted or polished, moldavite showcases a vibrant internal glow and a distinctive, slightly silky luster.

Highly prized for its extraterrestrial origin and unique beauty, moldavite has become a favorite among collectors. As a gemstone, it represents a literal fusion of terrestrial and cosmic forces, offering a piece of the universe.

Moonstone

RI	1.520–1.525	**Critical Angle**	41.6°
Birefringence	.005–008	**Cleavage**	Perfect in two directions
SG	2.56–2.59	**Heat sensitivity**	Moderate
Color	Varies	**Polish methods**	Cerium Oxide
Spectrum	Featureless	**Hardness**	6–6.5

Moonstone is a captivating gemstone from the feldspar group, celebrated for its ethereal glow known as adularescence—a floating, bluish or silvery light that appears to glide just beneath the surface of the stone. This optical phenomenon results from light scattering between thin, alternating layers of orthoclase and albite feldspar, giving moonstone its soft, moon-like sheen.

Moonstone has been admired since ancient times, with legends linking it to lunar deities and mystical powers. The Romans believed it was formed from solidified moonlight, and it has long been associated with intuition, femininity, and emotional balance. Traditionally found in Sri Lanka and India, moonstone is also sourced from Madagascar, Myanmar, Tanzania, and Brazil.

Its color range includes colorless, white, peach, gray, green, and occasionally brown or yellow tones. The finest moonstones are colorless, featuring a vivid blue adularescence and high transparency. These are typically cut en cabochon to enhance the glowing effect, although faceted examples exist for higher-clarity material.

With a Mohs hardness ranging from 6 to 6.5, moonstone is moderately soft and prone to cleavage, necessitating care during cutting, setting, and wear. It is frequently confused with other feldspar gems, such as rainbow moonstone (a labradorite variety with multicolored sheen) or sunstone; however, its gentle, floating light is distinctly recognizable.

Moonstone's exquisite beauty and symbolic significance make it a favorite among artisanal jewelry makers, spiritual enthusiasts, and admirers of luminous, naturally enchanting gems.

Obsidian

RI	1.450–1.550	**Critical Angle**	42.9°
Birefringence	None (Amorphous)	**Cleavage**	Conchoidal fracture
SG	2.3–2.6	**Heat sensitivity**	Yes
Color	Black, gray, brown, green	**Polish methods**	Cerium Oxide
Spectrum	None distinctive	**Hardness**	5–5.5

Obsidian is a volcanic glass formed from rapidly cooled lava and lacks a crystalline structure. Its name is believed to originate from the Roman explorer Obsidius, who supposedly discovered a similar material in Ethiopia. Obsidian typically appears black but can also display intriguing variations such as mahogany, snowflake, rainbow, and sheen types.

With its smooth, glassy texture and high reflectivity, obsidian has been used since prehistoric times for tools, weapons, and decorative items. In gemology, it is often cut into cabochons, beads, and carvings, showcasing its natural luster and striking, sometimes metallic effects.

Although relatively soft and brittle compared to crystalline gemstones, obsidian's beauty and historical significance make it a cherished material.

USGS (public domain)

Opal

RI	1.370–1.470	**Critical Angle**	43.2°
Birefringence	None (Amorphous)	**Cleavage**	None
SG	1.98–2.25	**Heat sensitivity**	Yes
Color	White, black, fire (orange-red), crystal (clear)	**Polish methods**	Cerium Oxide
Spectrum	Broad absorption under 500 nm (some types)	**Hardness**	5.5–6.5

Opal is a hydrated silica mineral revered for its mesmerizing play of color; an optical phenomenon caused by the diffraction of light through microscopic silica spheres. Its name likely originates from the Sanskrit upala, meaning "precious stone." Opal can range from fiery flashes of color against a dark background (black opal) to gentle pastel dances in lighter varieties (white or crystal opal).

Crystallizing in an amorphous structure, opal can display a body color that is white, black, gray, or any shade in between, while its play-of-color encompasses the entire visible spectrum. Precious opals stand apart from common opals, which do not exhibit this optical phenomenon.

Opal's symbolism spans cultures—it is associated with hope, purity, and creativity—and its fragility requires careful handling. Despite its sensitivity to impact, heat, and dryness, opal remains one of the most beloved and enchanting gemstones, celebrated for its unique, living brilliance that seems to hold all the colors of the universe within its delicate embrace.

While generally cut into cabochons, faceted opals can be exceedingly beautiful.

Oregon Sunstone

RI	1.560–1.572	**Critical Angle**	40.9°
Birefringence	.008–.010	**Cleavage**	Perfect in two directions
SG	2.62–2.68	**Heat sensitivity**	Moderate
Color	clear, yellow, champagne, pink, red, green, bi-color, tri-color	**Polish methods**	Cerium Oxide and Diamond
Spectrum	Featureless	**Hardness**	6–6.5

Oregon Sunstone is a unique and highly prized variety of feldspar found exclusively in the high-desert regions of southeastern Oregon, particularly in Lake and Harney counties. This gem belongs to the labradorite feldspar group and owes its fame to both its transparent clarity and its dazzling schiller effect—a metallic glitter caused by microscopic copper platelets suspended within the stone.

What makes Oregon Sunstone exceptional is that its color and shimmer are entirely natural—no treatments are used. Colors range from clear, champagne, pale yellow, and peach to richer tones of pink, red, green, and rare bi- or tri-color combinations. The most valuable examples display a combination of deep color and vibrant coppery flash. The copper inclusions can create a strong aventurescence (or glitter), distinguishing it from other feldspars around the world.

Legally, only material from Oregon can be marketed as "Oregon Sunstone." It is the official state gemstone of Oregon, and its limited locality adds to its desirability. The gem is typically faceted but is also found as beads and cabochons.

Oregon Sunstone has a hardness of approximately 6 to 6.5 on the Mohs scale, which makes it suitable for jewelry with protective settings. Because of its natural beauty, American origin, and untreated status, it is particularly popular among collectors, designers, and those seeking ethically sourced domestic gemstones.

Photo © Kell Hymer

Pearl

RI	1.530–1.685	**Critical Angle**	
Birefringence		**Cleavage**	None
SG	2.60–4.5	**Heat sensitivity**	High
Color	White, cream, pink, silver, gold, black, blue, green	**Polish methods**	Cerium Oxide
Spectrum	Featureless	**Hardness**	2.5–4.5

Pearl is one of the most iconic and enduring organic gemstones, cherished across cultures for millennia. Unlike mineral gems, pearls are formed biologically, produced within the soft tissue of mollusks when layers of aragonite and conchiolin build around a microscopic irritant. This layered structure gives rise to their signature luster, or "orient," a soft iridescence that has made pearls symbols of purity, elegance, and refinement throughout history.

Natural pearls were historically sourced from the Persian Gulf, Sri Lanka, and the Red Sea. However, today, the vast majority are cultured, grown under carefully controlled conditions in freshwater and saltwater farms, primarily in Japan, China, Australia, and French Polynesia. Pearls come in a wide range of natural colors, including white, cream, rose, gold, gray, and black, with treatments expanding the palette even further.

Despite their beauty, pearls are notably delicate. With a hardness of just 2.5 to 4.5, they are easily scratched and are highly sensitive to heat, chemicals, and dehydration. They require special care and are typically set in protective mountings. Pearls also differ in polish from other gems in that they are naturally polished. Albeit rare, they can be faceted into gemstones with extreme patience and care.

From ancient royalty to modern fashion, pearls remain a timeless gemstone, rich in symbolism and elegance. Whether natural or cultured, each pearl represents a unique creation of nature and time.

Photo © Darryl Alexander Somewhere In The Rainbow

Peridot

RI	1.650–1.703	**Critical Angle**	36.7°
Birefringence	0.035–0.038	**Cleavage**	Poor
SG	3.2–3.4	**Heat sensitivity**	No
Color	Olive green, yellow-green	**Polish methods**	Cerium Oxide and Diamond
Spectrum	Lines at 493, 453 nm	**Hardness**	6.5–7

Peridot, the gem variety of the mineral olivine, is one of the few gemstones that occur in only one color: a vibrant, grassy green. Its name is thought to derive from the Arabic faridat, meaning "gem." Historically, peridot has been treasured since ancient Egypt, where it was called the "gem of the sun" and mined on the island of Zabargad.

Peridot crystallizes in the orthorhombic system, formed deep within the Earth's mantle and brought to the surface through volcanic activity. Its green hue results from the presence of iron, and depending on its composition, it can range from yellow green to olive. With a strong double refraction, peridot can display a soft, velvety luster when expertly faceted.

Peridot's combination of durability and vibrant green color makes it a popular choice for various types of jewelry. Its glowing green continues to captivate with its earthy brilliance and cosmic origin, whether in ancient talismans or modern rings.

Photos © Peter Torraca.

Phenacite

RI	1.650–1.670	**Critical Angle**	37°
Birefringence	0.002	**Cleavage**	Indistinct
SG	2.9–3.0	**Heat sensitivity**	No
Color	Colorless, pale yellow	**Polish methods**	Aluminum Oxide and Diamond
Spectrum	Weak lines near 500 nm	**Hardness**	7.5–8

Phenacite (also spelled phenakite) is a rare beryllium silicate mineral prized for its exceptional brilliance and near diamond-like luster. Its name comes from the Greek phenakos, meaning "deceiver," because its appearance often mimics that of quartz. Crystallizing in the trigonal system, phenacite typically forms prismatic crystals with excellent clarity.

When faceted, phenacite exhibits extraordinary brilliance and can appear almost ice-like, showcasing a bright, vitreous luster. While it typically occurs colorless, it can also display pale hues of yellow, pink, or green depending on trace elements. Transparent phenacite crystals are rare, and large faceted stones are particularly valued by collectors.

Phenacite holds metaphysical associations with heightened consciousness and spiritual awakening. Due to its optical excellence and rarity, it has become a coveted gem among those seeking unusual alternatives to traditional colorless stones. Whether admired for its cutting challenges or luminous purity, phenacite remains a shining example of nature's understated beauty.

Prehnite

RI	1.610–1.669	**Critical Angle**	38.2°
Birefringence	0.0059	**Cleavage**	Distinct in one direction
SG	2.9–3.0	**Heat sensitivity**	Yes
Color	Green, yellow-green, white	**Polish methods**	Cerium Oxide
Spectrum	Weak absorption below 500 nm	**Hardness**	6–6.5

Prehnite is a hydrous calcium aluminum silicate mineral renowned for its soothing green to yellow-green hue and gentle glow. It was named after Colonel Hendrik von Prehn, a Dutch mineralogist and explorer, and was one of the first minerals named after a person.

Crystallizing in the orthorhombic system, prehnite often forms in botryoidal, stalactitic, or granular habits; however, rare facetable crystals are found in pegmatites and basalt cavities. Prehnite's luster can range from vitreous to pearly, and transparent to translucent stones are highly desirable for collectors and jewelry designers.

When faceted or carved, it emits a soft, luminous glow that feels both grounded and ethereal. Although smoother than many mainstream gemstones, careful handling allows prehnite's calming beauty to shine. As both a jewelry stone and a collector's gem, prehnite offers a peaceful, inviting charm that resonates with the heart.

Photo © Rob Lavinsky, iRocks.com

Quartz

RI	1.544–1.553	**Critical Angle**	40.5°
Birefringence	0.009	**Cleavage**	None
SG	2.65	**Heat sensitivity**	No
Color	Colorless, purple (amethyst), yellow (citrine), pink (rose quartz), smoky	**Polish methods**	Cerium Oxide or Tin Oxide
Spectrum	None or very weak at 460 nm (some varieties)	**Hardness**	7

Quartz is one of the most abundant and versatile minerals on Earth. It is composed of silicon dioxide (SiO_2). Its name likely derives from the old German word "quarz," meaning "hard," reflecting its notable durability. Quartz crystallizes in the hexagonal system and forms in a dazzling array of environments, including igneous and metamorphic rocks as well as hydrothermal veins.

As a gemstone, quartz appears in countless varieties: amethyst, citrine, smoky quartz, rose quartz, rock crystal, and more. Its ability to take on color from trace elements or radiation exposure results in a full rainbow of gem types. Quartz's strong luster, relative hardness, and affordability make it a popular choice for jewelry, carvings, and ornamental objects.

Its combination of widespread availability, diverse forms, and stunning visual effects ensures that quartz remains one of the most cherished and extensively used gemstones in human history.

Macrocrystalline Quartz (Visible Crystals)

Amethyst

- Color: Purple to violet
- Traits: Iron-bearing quartz; color fades in sunlight; heat-treated to citrine
- Hardness: 7.0
- Rarity: Common (high-quality material may be Uncommon)

Citrine

- Color: Yellow to orange to brownish
- Traits: Heat-treated amethyst or smoky quartz; natural citrine is much rarer
- Hardness: 7.0
- Rarity: Common (natural citrine: Rare)

Ametrine

- Color: Purple and yellow/orange in the same crystal
- Traits: Natural bi-color quartz; most material from Bolivia
- Hardness: 7.0
- Rarity: Rare

Smoky Quartz

- Color: Light brown to black
- Traits: Irradiated aluminum in crystal; very stable and often large
- Hardness: 7.0
- Rarity: Common

Rock Crystal

- Color: Colorless and transparent
- Traits: Pure quartz; historically used for carvings and lenses
- Hardness: 7.0
- Rarity: Common

Rose Quartz

- Color: Pink to rosy pink
- Traits: Often translucent to opaque; color caused by titanium or manganese; usually cabbed
- Hardness: 7.0
- Rarity: Common (transparent material: Very Rare)

Prasiolite

- Color: Light green
- Traits: Heat-treated amethyst or natural in rare cases; also called green amethyst (discouraged)
- Hardness: 7.0
- Rarity: Uncommon

Rhodochrosite

RI	1.600–1.820	**Critical Angle**	37°
Birefringence	0.22	**Cleavage**	Perfect
SG	3.5–3.7	**Heat sensitivity**	Yes
Color	Pink, red, white	**Polish methods**	Cerium Oxide
Spectrum	Broad band at 540–560 nm	**Hardness**	3.5–4

Rhodochrosite is a manganese carbonate mineral celebrated for its luscious pink to red hues and banded patterns. Its name derives from the Greek rhodos ("rose") and chroma ("color"), perfectly capturing its distinctive coloration. Found in hydrothermal veins and manganese deposits, rhodochrosite crystallizes in the trigonal system, often forming rhombohedral crystals or massive, banded aggregates.

Gem-quality rhodochrosite is generally translucent to opaque, although transparent crystals suitable for faceting have been discovered in regions such as Colorado and Argentina. When cut, rhodochrosite showcases a soft, vitreous luster and a striking internal glow; however, its relative softness and perfect cleavage necessitate careful handling.

Long valued by collectors and increasingly appreciated in fine jewelry, its mesmerizing color, gentle beauty, and profound connection to human emotions make it one of the most cherished pink stones in the mineral world.

Photo © Stephen Kotlowski

Rutile

RI	2.616–2.903	**Critical Angle**	31.2°
Birefringence	0.287	**Cleavage**	Good
SG	4.2–4.3	**Heat sensitivity**	No
Color	Red, brown, golden, black	**Polish methods**	Aluminum Oxide and Diamond
Spectrum	None distinctive	**Hardness**	6–6.5

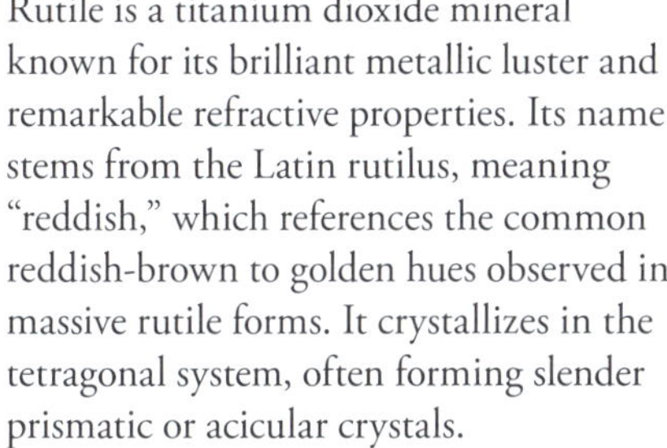

Rutile is a titanium dioxide mineral known for its brilliant metallic luster and remarkable refractive properties. Its name stems from the Latin rutilus, meaning "reddish," which references the common reddish-brown to golden hues observed in massive rutile forms. It crystallizes in the tetragonal system, often forming slender prismatic or acicular crystals.

While pure rutile crystals can be faceted into gemstones, the mineral is perhaps most famous for the needle-like inclusions it creates within other stones—such as rutilated quartz—forming mesmerizing internal landscapes of golden threads. Faceted rutile itself displays an exceptional adamantine luster and strong pleochroism.

Whether admired as delicate needles dancing within quartz or as sparkling, faceted stones, rutile's captivating internal fireworks provide a striking glimpse into the dynamic beauty of the microscopic world.

Photo © Tom Schultz

Scapolite

RI	1.540–1.579	**Critical Angle**	40°
Birefringence	0.006–0.020	**Cleavage**	Perfect in one direction
SG	2.5–2.8	**Heat sensitivity**	Moderate
Color	Colorless, white, yellow, violet, pink	**Polish methods**	Cerium Oxide and Diamond
Spectrum	Varies by type—can show band at 480 nm	**Hardness**	5.5–6

Scapolite is a series of silicate minerals that bridges the gap between marialite (sodium-rich) and meionite (calcium-rich) compositions. Its name comes from the Greek word skapos, meaning "stick" or "shaft," referring to its elongated prismatic crystals. Scapolite typically forms in metamorphic environments such as contact or regionally metamorphosed rocks.

Gem-quality scapolite occurs in various colors, including yellow, violet, pink, brown, and gray. It crystallizes in the tetragonal system and, when properly faceted, exhibits excellent clarity and a bright, vitreous luster. Some scapolite stones display chatoyancy, producing rare and highly valued cat's-eye effects.

Although relatively soft compared to many traditional gemstones, scapolite's vibrant colors and optical properties make it a favorite among collectors and designers seeking something unique. In gem form, scapolite offers a sparkling, lesser-known alternative for those looking to move beyond the conventional.

Cut gem © Dan Lynch. rough gem: public domain.

Sphalerite

RI	2.368–2.371	**Critical Angle**	25.3°
Birefringence	0.003	**Cleavage**	Perfect
SG	3.9–4.2	**Heat sensitivity**	Yes
Color	Brown, yellow, red, black	**Polish methods**	Cerium Oxide
Spectrum	None distinctive	**Hardness**	3.5–4

Sphalerite is a zinc sulfide mineral celebrated for its brilliant luster and exceptional dispersion, surpassing even that of diamond. Its name derives from the Greek term sphaleros, meaning "treacherous," due to its challenging identification during early mining endeavors.

Crystallizing in the isometric system, sphalerite typically appears in shades of yellow, brown, red, green, and black, depending on its iron content. Transparent, gem-quality sphalerite is rare and displays a fiery kaleidoscope of internal flashes when it is faceted. However, its softness and perfect cleavage make it best suited for display by collectors rather than for use in jewelry.

A properly cut sphalerite is one of the most visually thrilling gems for collectors, embodying the fiery brilliance hidden within the Earth's crust.

Sphene

RI	1.843–2.110	**Critical Angle**	32.5°
Birefringence	0.267	**Cleavage**	Distinct
SG	3.5–3.6	**Heat sensitivity**	Yes
Color	Green, yellow, brown, orange	**Polish methods**	Cerium Oxide and Diamond
Spectrum	Broad band at 480 nm	**Hardness**	5–5.5

Sphene, more properly known as titanite, is a calcium titanium silicate recognized for its extraordinary fire and brilliant dispersion. The name "sphene" comes from the Greek sphen, meaning "wedge," which describes its typical crystal habit.

Crystallizing in the monoclinic system, sphene often displays vivid green, yellow, or brown hues and exhibits strong pleochroism, shifting colors as the gem is turned. Well-cut sphene stones dazzle with rainbow flashes of color under light, rivaling even a diamond's dispersion.

Despite its stunning optical properties, sphene's relative softness necessitates careful handling. For collectors and gem enthusiasts, a fine sphene represents one of nature's brightest and most lively spectacles.

Rough gem © Kell Hymer, Cut gem © Dan Lynch

Spinel

RI	1.712–1.736	**Critical Angle**	41.4°
Birefringence	None (Isotropic)	**Cleavage**	None
SG	3.5–4.1	**Heat sensitivity**	No
Color	Red, pink, blue, violet, orange, black	**Polish methods**	Aluminum Oxide and Diamond
Spectrum	Broad band around 460 nm (blue/red types)	**Hardness**	7.5–8

Spinel is a magnesium aluminum oxide mineral that has often been historically mistaken for ruby or sapphire. Its name likely comes from the Latin word spina, meaning "thorn," which references its pointed crystal habit. Found in metamorphic rocks and alluvial deposits, spinel crystallizes in the isometric system.

Gem spinel occurs in a dazzling array of colors: red, pink, blue, violet, lavender, orange, and even gray. When properly faceted, transparent crystals reveal a bright luster and excellent durability. Unlike corundum, spinel is singly refractive, resulting in pure, saturated color without pleochroism.

Today, spinel is finally receiving the appreciation it deserves, celebrated for its vivid hues, historical significance, and untreated natural beauty. Spinel is a gemstone that embodies both timeless elegance and modern rediscovery.

Spodumene

RI	1.648–1.680	**Critical Angle**	36.8°
Birefringence	0.014–0.016	**Cleavage**	Perfect in two directions
SG	3.1–3.2	**Heat sensitivity**	Yes (kunzite fades)
Color	Pink (kunzite), green (hiddenite), colorless	**Polish methods**	Cerium Oxide and Diamond
Spectrum	Weak bands below 500 nm	**Hardness**	6.5–7

Spodumene is a lithium aluminum silicate mineral most renowned for its gem varieties, kunzite (pink to violet) and hiddenite (green). The name is derived from the Greek word spodumenos, meaning "burnt to ashes," which refers to its typical ashen-gray appearance in massive form.

Crystallizing in the monoclinic system, spodumene often forms large, well-terminated crystals. When cut, transparent crystals produce gems of remarkable clarity and brilliance. Kunzite is prized for its delicate pink hues, while hiddenite showcases vibrant green tones due to its chromium content.

Though beautiful, spodumene's perfect cleavage requires careful cutting and handling. Whether pale and delicate or vivid and lively, spodumene gems provide a luminous, romantic presence.

Cut gem: Didier Descouens (CC BY-SA 3.0), Rough gem: Public domain

Sulfur

RI	1.957–2.245	**Critical Angle**	30.8°
Birefringence	0.288	**Cleavage**	Poor
SG	2.0–2.1	**Heat sensitivity**	Yes
Color	Bright Yellow	**Polish methods**	Cerium Oxide
Spectrum	None distinctive	**Hardness**	1.5–2.5

Sulfur, an elemental mineral, is best known for its bright yellow color and distinctive odor when burned. Historically recognized since ancient times, its name stems from the Latin *sulphurium*. Sulfur forms near volcanic vents, hot springs, and evaporite deposits, crystallizing in the orthorhombic system.

While sulfur crystals can be striking in appearance—radiating golden or lemon-yellow hues—they are also

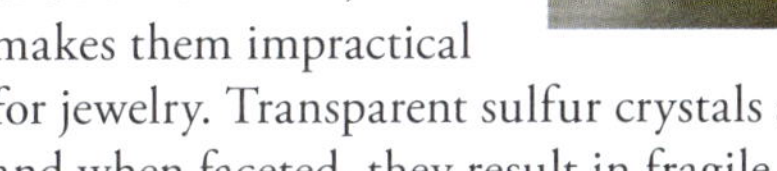

extremely soft, brittle, and heat-sensitive, which makes them impractical for jewelry. Transparent sulfur crystals are rare, and when faceted, they result in fragile gems with a soft, waxy luster.

Although it is primarily a mineral rather than a gemological staple, sulfur's vivid color and ancient significance give it a fascinating, albeit delicate, place among Earth's natural wonders.

Photos © Scott Sucher

Tanzanite

RI	1.685–1.707	**Critical Angle**	40.5°
Birefringence	0.008–0.013	**Cleavage**	Distince in one direction
SG	3.85	**Heat sensitivity**	Moderate to High
Color	Violet-blue, blue, violet, brownish	**Polish methods**	Aluminum Oxide, Diamond
Spectrum	Weak bands in violet and blue	**Hardness**	7

Tanzanite is the most celebrated and valuable variety of the zoisite family, prized for its striking color and rarity. Discovered in 1967 in the Merelani Hills of northern Tanzania, it remains one of the few gemstones in the world sourced almost entirely from a single location. Naturally trichroic, unheated tanzanite displays three distinct colors—blue, violet, and burgundy—depending on the viewing angle. However, nearly all tanzanite sold today is gently heat-treated to eliminate brownish tones and enhance its vibrant blue and violet hues, making it visually comparable to the finest sapphires, but with a softer, velvetier luster.

Tanzanite crystals typically grow in long, prismatic shapes with distinct striations, making them ideal for cutting into elongated designs such as cushions, pears, and ovals that highlight their brilliance and rich body color. Despite their beauty, tanzanite is relatively delicate compared to other major gems, prone to cleaving when struck and sensitive to temperature changes. Proper handling, careful setting, and avoidance of ultrasonic cleaning are crucial to preserving its allure.

The discovery of tanzanite captured global attention almost instantly, with Tiffany & Co. helping to popularize it internationally. Its dazzling color and relative affordability compared to sapphire fueled its rise as a favorite for fine jewelry and collectors. With its vivid hues and compelling story, tanzanite continues to enchant gem enthusiasts and jewelers worldwide.

Cut gem © Roger Dery, Rough gem © Peter Torraca

Topaz

RI	1.609–1.643	**Critical Angle**	38.2°
Birefringence	0.014	**Cleavage**	Perfect in one direction
SG	3.4–3.6	**Heat sensitivity**	Yes (can fade)
Color	Colorless, blue, yellow, pink, brown	**Polish methods**	Cerium Oxide and Diamond
Spectrum	None or weak absorption below 460 nm	**Hardness**	8

Topaz is a fluorosilicate mineral renowned for its brilliance, vibrant range of colors, and impressive hardness. Its name may derive from the Sanskrit tapas (meaning "fire") or the ancient Greek Topazios, the name of an island in the Red Sea. Topaz crystallizes in the orthorhombic system and often forms large, prismatic crystals with perfect basal cleavage.

Naturally occurring topaz is usually colorless, but impurities can create shades of blue, pink, yellow, orange, brown, or even rare red. Blue topaz is particularly popular today, often produced through irradiation and heat treatment. When faceted, topaz displays a bright vitreous luster and excellent clarity.

Its durability, along with its wide color palette, ensures that topaz remains one of the most versatile and cherished gemstones for both jewelry enthusiasts and collectors.

Tourmaline

RI	1.614–1.666	**Critical Angle**	37.7°
Birefringence	0.018–0.040	**Cleavage**	Indistinct
SG	3.0–3.3	**Heat sensitivity**	No
Color	Green, pink, blue, yellow, black	**Polish methods**	Aluminum Oxide and Diamond
Spectrum	Lines at 458, 498, 520, 640 nm (varies)	**Hardness**	7–7.5

Tourmaline is a complex boron silicate mineral that occurs in an astonishing variety of colors, sometimes even within the same crystal. Its name comes from the Sinhalese word turmali, meaning "mixed gems," which reflects its colorful diversity. Tourmaline crystallizes in the trigonal system, often forming slender, prismatic crystals.

Gem-quality tourmaline can range from vivid pinks and reds (rubellite) to greens (verdelite) and blues (indicolite), as well as to stunning bi-colored or tri-colored forms like watermelon tourmaline. Some tourmaline varieties also exhibit a cat's-eye effect or strong pleochroism. With its good hardness and dazzling range, tourmaline is a favorite among jewelers and collectors alike.

In metaphysical lore, tourmaline is associated with protection, grounding, and emotional healing, with its varied colors offering different energetic attributes. Whether admired for its vibrant hues or symbolic richness, tourmaline stands as one of the most beloved and dynamic gemstone families.

Zincite

RI	2.013–2.029	**Critical Angle**	37.3°
Birefringence	0.016	**Cleavage**	None
SG	5.7–6.4	**Heat sensitivity**	Yes
Color	Red, orange, yellow	**Polish methods**	Cerium Oxide
Spectrum	None distinctive	**Hardness**	4

Zincite is a rare mineral form of zinc oxide, typically appearing as vibrant red, orange, or yellow crystals. Natural zincite is exceedingly rare and is primarily found in association with zinc ore bodies, such as those in Poland and New Jersey. However, synthetic zincite crystals have been produced accidentally during smelting processes since the 19th century.

Crystallizing in the hexagonal system, zincite is highly lustrous and visually dynamic, with transparent specimens displaying intense internal fire and vivid coloration. When faceted, zincite reveals extraordinary brilliance but remains extremely soft and fragile, limiting its use to collector's pieces rather than wearable jewelry.

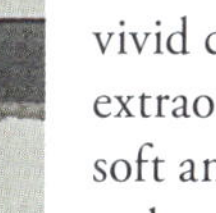

Although fragile, zincite offers a dramatic presence and stands as a testament to both human ingenuity and nature's unexpected artistic expressions.

Zircon

RI	1.810–2.024	**Critical Angle**	38.9°
Birefringence	0.059–0.078	**Cleavage**	Poor
SG	3.9–4.8	**Heat sensitivity**	No
Color	Colorless, brown, yellow, green, blue	**Polish methods**	Cerium Oxide or Diamond Paste
Spectrum	Lines at 653, 683, 693 nm (high type)	**Hardness**	6–7.5

Zircon is a zirconium silicate mineral prized for its exceptional brilliance, fire, and ancient geological heritage. Its name likely stems from the Persian word "zargun," meaning "gold-colored." Zircon crystallizes in the tetragonal system and is found in various geological settings, from igneous rocks to metamorphic deposits.

Zircon comes in a stunning range of colors—blue, golden yellow, green, brown, pink, and colorless—often enhanced by heat treatment. Its high refractive index and strong dispersion give cut zircon a fire comparable to that of a diamond, although zircon's double refraction can produce a charming "doubling" of facets when viewed closely.

Zircon is one of the Earth's oldest minerals, with some crystals dating back over 4 billion years. Although it is sometimes confused with synthetic cubic zirconia, natural zircon possesses its own unmistakable charm and durability. As a gemstone, zircon combines ancient origins, vivid color, and brilliant optical performance, earning a distinguished place in both fine jewelry and mineral collections.

Zoisite

RI	1.685–1.707	**Critical Angle**	40.5°
Birefringence	0.008–0.013	**Cleavage**	Distince in one direction
SG	3.85	**Heat sensitivity**	Moderate to High
Color	Violet-blue, blue, violet, brownish	**Polish methods**	Aluminum Oxide and Diamond
Spectrum	Weak bands in violet and blue	**Hardness**	7

Zoisite is a beautiful and versatile mineral species belonging to the epidote group. It was first discovered in the Saualpe region of Austria in 1805 and named in honor of the mineralogist Sigmund Zois. Crystallizing in the orthorhombic system, zoisite forms elongated, often striated crystals that can display a captivating range of colors depending on trace impurities. The most famous variety, tanzanite, was uncovered only in 1967 near Mount Kilimanjaro in Tanzania and has since become one of the most celebrated gemstones in the world. Naturally trichroic, tanzanite displays distinct blue, violet, and burgundy hues from different viewing angles, though most tanzanite on the market is heat-treated to enhance its vivid blue and violet tones.

Beyond tanzanite, zoisite is found in vibrant green varieties, especially when colored by chromium. Chrome zoisite, although often opaque, can occasionally yield transparent crystals of exceptional beauty. Another notable form is anyolite, an ornamental material where vivid green zoisite showcases striking ruby crystals, creating a dramatic and colorful effect that is popular for carvings and metaphysical objects. While zoisite offers remarkable color and vibrancy, it is generally less durable than many traditional gemstones, necessitating careful handling to avoid scratches or damage during wear.

Zoisite's rich colors and rare optical phenomena have made it highly sought after by both collectors and jewelers. Whether fashioned into a brilliant tanzanite or a sculptural ruby-in-zoisite carving, zoisite stands as one of nature's most enchanting creations.

Cut gem © Dan Lynch, Rough gem: Rob Lavinsky, iRocks.com

Synthetic Gem Species

Synthetic Alexandrite

RI	1.746–1.755	**Critical Angle**	37.6°
Birefringence	0.008–0.010	**Cleavage**	Distinct
SG	3.7–3.8	**Heat sensitivity**	No
Color	Green to red (color-change)	**Polish methods**	Aluminum Oxide and Diamond
Spectrum	Lines at 443, 460, 680 nm	**Hardness**	8.5

Synthetic alexandrite is a laboratory-created form of chrysoberyl ($BeAl_2O_4$) that replicates the natural stone's remarkable color-change effect. It is primarily produced through the Czochralski pulling method or the floating zone process, allowing for careful control over chemical composition and crystal structure.

Synthetic alexandrite crystallizes in the orthorhombic system and displays the same pleochroism and dramatic color shifts as natural alexandrite—typically changing from bluish green in daylight to purplish red under incandescent light. Synthetic varieties tend to have cleaner, more vivid color transitions than their often inclusion-rich natural counterparts. Their hardness, brilliance, and durability match those of natural chrysoberyl.

Thanks to its relative affordability and stunning optical properties, synthetic alexandrite is popular for fine jewelry, particularly in rings and pendants. Metaphysically, it symbolizes change, intuition, and inner growth. As a gemstone, synthetic alexandrite provides a breathtaking, accessible experience of one of nature's most prized optical phenomena, all made possible through human artistry.

Synthetic Aquamarine

RI	1.577–1.583	**Critical Angle**	39.3°
Birefringence	0.005	**Cleavage**	Poor
SG	2.68–2.80	**Heat sensitivity**	Moderate
Color	Light blue, greenish-blue	**Polish methods**	Cerium Oxide and Diamond
Spectrum	Broad bands at 430, 456 nm	**Hardness**	7.5–8

Synthetic aquamarine is a laboratory-grown variety of beryl ($Be_3Al_2Si_6O_{18}$), designed to replicate the serene blue color of natural aquamarine. It is primarily produced using hydrothermal synthesis, in which a beryllium-containing solution is heated under high pressure to promote slow, natural-like crystal growth. Hydrothermal synthetic aquamarine offers excellent optical clarity and minimal inclusions, often outperforming natural stones in transparency.

Crystallizing in the hexagonal system, synthetic aquamarine exhibits the same physical properties as its natural counterpart—good toughness, vitreous luster, and characteristic pale to medium blue coloration caused by iron impurities. The synthetic version typically lacks the zoning and internal flaws found in many natural aquamarines, offering more consistent color and brilliance.

Synthetic aquamarine offers an attractive alternative for jewelry, blending the calming beauty of the sea-colored gem with enhanced clarity and durability. It retains the metaphysical associations of peace, emotional balance, and communication often linked to natural aquamarine. For those desiring the beauty of aquamarine without the premium price or imperfections, synthetic aquamarine presents a stunning and accessible option.

Synthetic Corundum

RI	1.762–1.770	**Critical Angle**	34.4°
Birefringence	0.008	**Cleavage**	None
SG	3.9–4.1	**Heat sensitivity**	No
Color	Colorless, red (ruby), blue (sapphire), yellow, green, pink	**Polish methods**	Diamond
Spectrum	Fine lines at 470, 660 nm (varies by dopant)	**Hardness**	9

Synthetic corundum—comprising synthetic ruby and sapphire—is produced using various manufacturing methods, most notably the Verneuil flame fusion process, flux growth, and Czochralski pulling. Flame fusion, developed in the early 1900s, melts aluminum oxide powder and allows it to crystallize onto a rotating rod, rapidly and affordably creating vibrant, flawless crystals.

Synthetic corundum is chemically identical to natural sapphire and ruby (Al_2O_3) and crystallizes in the trigonal system. The synthetic versions can be produced in a rainbow of colors by doping with trace elements like chromium (for red ruby), iron, and titanium (for blue sapphire), or vanadium (for purple hues). Synthetic stones exhibit exceptional hardness (9 on the Mohs scale), durability, and a vitreous luster, often outperforming natural stones in clarity and color saturation.

Synthetic corundum has revolutionized the jewelry industry by making high-quality gems accessible to a broader market. These gems are prized for their brilliance, toughness, and affordability, and they are also widely used in industrial applications. Although specialists can easily identify them through growth patterns and inclusions, synthetic corundum remains a celebrated achievement in gem technology, offering enduring beauty shaped by human mastery.

Cubic Zirconia (CZ)

RI	2.150–2.180	**Critical Angle**	28.5°
Birefringence	None (Isotropic)	**Cleavage**	None
SG	5.5–6.0	**Heat sensitivity**	No
Color	Colorless, yellow, pink, blue, green	**Polish methods**	Diamond
Spectrum	None distinctive	**Hardness**	8–8.5

Cubic zirconia (CZ) is a synthetic crystalline form of zirconium dioxide (ZrO_2), engineered to be a brilliant, affordable diamond simulant. Originally developed in Soviet laboratories in the 1970s for laser optics, CZ became a dominant force in the jewelry market due to its exceptional brilliance, fire, and affordability. It is manufactured through the skull melting method, in which powdered zirconium dioxide is melted in a controlled environment and crystallized into flawless boules.

Crystallizing in the isometric system, cubic zirconia is typically colorless but can be doped with trace elements to produce a range of colors, including yellow, pink, green, and blue. It exhibits high dispersion (fire) and a hardness of about 8 to 8.5 on the Mohs scale, although it is softer and denser than diamond.

Cubic zirconia offers stunning optical performance at a fraction of the cost of diamond, making it a popular choice for engagement rings, earrings, and fashion jewelry. It symbolizes clarity, practicality, and adaptability. Although it can be distinguished from diamond by weight, heat conductivity, and minor optical differences, cubic zirconia remains one of the most successful and beloved synthetic gems in the modern jewelry world.

Cut gem © Greg Phillips, Rough gem © Tom Schultz

Synthetic Emerald

RI	1.565–1.602	Critical Angle	41.1°
Birefringence	0.006–0.009	Cleavage	Poor
SG	2.68–2.78	Heat sensitivity	Yes
Color	Green, bluish-green	Polish methods	Cerium Oxide and Diamond
Spectrum	Lines at 683, 683.5, 561 nm	Hardness	7.5–8

Synthetic emeralds are laboratory-created beryllium aluminum silicates ($Be_3Al_2Si_6O_{18}$) that replicate the composition and appearance of natural emeralds. They are typically produced using hydrothermal or flux-growth methods. Hydrothermal emeralds grow in a sealed vessel filled with water and mineral components under high temperature and pressure, while flux-grown emeralds crystallize from a molten flux solution that reduces the melting point and promotes slow crystal growth.

These synthetic emeralds crystallize in the hexagonal system and possess the same vibrant green hues, refractive indices, and specific gravity as natural emeralds. Their color is typically achieved through chromium or vanadium doping. Visually, synthetic emeralds are highly convincing, often exhibiting fewer fractures and superior clarity compared to their natural counterparts, although characteristic growth features (such as curved striae or tiny flux inclusions) can reveal their origin under magnification.

Synthetic emeralds provide a more affordable and durable alternative to fragile natural emeralds, making them popular choices for fine jewelry. They possess the same metaphysical associations with growth, rebirth, and wisdom. With their rich green hues and enhanced clarity, hydrothermal and flux-grown emeralds represent a brilliant fusion of nature's chemistry and human ingenuity.

Photos © Gems of Science

Gadolinium Gallium Garnet (GGG)

RI	1.950–1.970
Birefringence	None (Isotropic)
SG	7.05
Color	Colorless, yellow, green
Spectrum	None distinctive

Critical Angle	31.2°
Cleavage	None
Heat sensitivity	No
Polish methods	Diamond
Hardness	6.5–7

Gadolinium gallium garnet (GGG, $Gd_3Ga_5O_{12}$) is another synthetic garnet material primarily developed for optical and laser applications, but it is also utilized in jewelry. It is grown using the Czochralski method, which allows for the production of large, high-quality crystals. Originally introduced in the 1970s, GGG briefly served as a diamond simulant before being overtaken by cubic zirconia.

GGG crystallizes in the isometric system and is typically colorless or pale yellow but can be doped with various elements to produce blue, green, or pink hues. It has a hardness of approximately 6.5 to 7.5 and a high refractive index, giving it excellent brilliance and light performance. However, it is softer and heavier than diamond.

Today, GGG is more commonly found among collectors and vintage jewelry enthusiasts. Metaphysically, it is associated with transformation and creative energy. As a gemstone, gadolinium gallium garnet captures a fascinating moment in gemological history—a testament to the ongoing quest for perfection through human innovation.

Glass

RI	1.45–1.70	**Critical Angle**	42-47°
Birefringence	None	**Cleavage**	None
SG	2.2–4.6	**Heat sensitivity**	High
Color	Any color	**Polish methods**	Cerium Oxide
Spectrum	Broad with no distinct absorption lines	**Hardness**	6

Glass has played a critical role in the history of adornment and gemstone simulation for over 3,000 years. Unlike natural minerals, glass is an amorphous, non-crystalline substance formed by the rapid cooling of molten silica mixed with other stabilizing compounds. Early civilizations, such as those in Egypt and Mesopotamia, pioneered decorative glasswork, creating beads and inlays that mimicked prized gems like turquoise, lapis lazuli, and emerald. Today, synthetic glass remains a widely accessible and versatile material in the realm of gemstones and faceting.

In gem-cutting, glass is valued for its ease of shaping, availability in a wide range of colors, and structural consistency. One popular form is the x-cube (or X-shaped cube) rough, which features pre-aligned planes that are ideal for standard and fantasy cuts. Since glass lacks internal cleavage and crystalline constraints, faceters can experiment freely with facet patterns and artistic designs. However, cutters must be cautious of its relatively low hardness (≈5–6 on the Mohs scale) and sensitivity to heat and pressure, as over-polishing or aggressive dopping can lead to fractures or crazing.

High-lead-content glass, also known as lead crystal, exhibits greater brilliance due to a higher refractive index (1.50–1.70) and is often used in precision-cut diamond simulants. While it lacks the inherent rarity and durability of true gemstones, glass holds a valuable position in both traditional and contemporary lapidary arts, particularly as a training material and a medium for custom, exhibition-grade faceting projects.

Photos ©Dan Lynch

Lutetium Aluminum Garnet (LuAG)

RI	1.83	**Critical Angle**	32.3°
Birefringence	0.004	**Cleavage**	No
SG	6.7	**Heat sensitivity**	No
Color	Various	**Polish methods**	Aluminium Oxide and Diamond
Spectrum	–	**Hardness**	6.5–7

Lutetium Aluminum Garnet (LuAG) is a synthetic garnet primarily designed for advanced optical applications, but it is increasingly appreciated in the gem-cutting world for its exceptional properties. Composed of lutetium, aluminum, and oxygen, it crystallizes in the isometric system, presenting high symmetry ideal for faceting. Although not naturally occurring, LuAG's optical and physical characteristics rival or even exceed many natural gemstones.

LuAG exhibits a high refractive index of approximately 1.83, which contributes to its excellent brilliance when properly faceted. It has a Mohs hardness of 8.5, making it suitable for jewelry; however, its rarity and synthetic origin often place it in the realm of collectors and faceting enthusiasts. The material is typically colorless to pale yellow or light green, featuring strong dispersion and minimal inclusions.

Originally developed for laser host crystals and scintillator detectors, LuAG's entry into the gem world is recent and limited. Its high density (6.7 g/cm^3) and precise optical behavior make it appealing for specialty faceting projects. While not marketed as a gem material on a large scale, LuAG represents a fascinating example of how synthetic materials with industrial origins are finding creative expression in the lapidary arts.

Photos © Gems of Science

Synthetic Moissanite

RI	2.648–2.691	**Critical Angle**	24.5°
Birefringence	0.043	**Cleavage**	None
SG	3.2	**Heat sensitivity**	No
Color	Colorless, greenish, near-colorless	**Polish methods**	Diamond
Spectrum	None distinctive	**Hardness**	9.25

Synthetic moissanite is a laboratory-grown form of silicon carbide (SiC), created as a dazzling alternative to diamonds. While natural moissanite is extremely rare—originally discovered in meteorites—synthetic production began in the late 20th century through a complex and time-consuming process that involves controlled crystal growth at high temperatures and pressures.

Synthetic moissanite crystallizes in the hexagonal system and exhibits exceptional optical properties, including a refractive index higher than that of diamond and extraordinary fire (dispersion). With a Mohs hardness of 9.25, it ranks among the hardest known gemstones suitable for daily wear. Typically, colorless to near-colorless, modern moissanite can also be produced in yellow, green, blue, and gray tones.

Moissanite is cherished for its brilliance, durability, and affordability. It is highly resistant to scratching, chipping, and heat, making it ideal for engagement rings and fine jewelry. Its metaphysical associations include inner strength, clarity, and connection to cosmic energy, reflecting its extraterrestrial origins. Offering unmatched sparkle and resilience, synthetic moissanite represents one of the greatest achievements in creating a high-performance, ethical, and visually stunning gemstone.

Rough gem © Toms Box of Rocks, Cut gem © Gems of Science

Synthetic Opal

RI	1.370–1.470	**Critical Angle**	43.2°
Birefringence	None (Amorphous)	**Cleavage**	None
SG	1.98–2.25	**Heat sensitivity**	Yes
Color	White, black, crystal, fire colors	**Polish methods**	Cerium Oxide
Spectrum	Broad absorption under 500 nm	**Hardness**	5.5–6.5

Synthetic opal is a laboratory-created form of hydrated silica ($SiO_2 \cdot nH_2O$) that mimics the structure, chemistry, and brilliant play of color of natural opal. Unlike many synthetic gems formed by flame fusion or hydrothermal methods, synthetic opal is produced through a slow sedimentation process. Silica spheres of uniform size are allowed to settle over extended periods, arranging themselves into a tight, orderly structure that produces the characteristic diffraction pattern seen as opal's fire.

Synthetic opal retains the same basic physical structure as natural opal but typically has fewer inclusions and exhibits a more uniform color play. It is often distinguishable by its more regular patterns, brighter colors, and the absence of the water content variations found in natural stones. It crystallizes in an amorphous structure and displays a hardness of approximately 5.5–6.5 on the Mohs scale.

Synthetic opals come in a dazzling array of colors—white, blue, green, pink, and black—and are available in both precious (play-of-color) and common (no play-of-color) forms. They are valued for their affordability, durability improvements (especially in stabilized forms), and striking beauty. Metaphysically, opal is linked with creativity, spontaneity, and emotional amplification, whether natural or synthetic. Synthetic opal offers an accessible and colorful connection to one of the Earth's most captivating visual phenomena.

Photos © Dan Lynch

Synthetic Quartz

RI	1.544–1.553	**Critical Angle**	40.5°
Birefringence	0.009	**Cleavage**	None
SG	2.65	**Heat sensitivity**	No
Color	Colorless, pink, yellow, purple, smoky	**Polish methods**	Cerium Oxide
Spectrum	Weak line at 460 nm (varies)	**Hardness**	7

Synthetic quartz is laboratory-grown silicon dioxide (SiO_2) that is chemically identical to natural quartz. It is primarily produced through the hydrothermal growth process, during which silicon dioxide dissolves in a high-pressure, high-temperature aqueous solution and recrystallizes onto seed plates over weeks or months. This method mimics the natural formation of quartz deep within the Earth but under strictly controlled conditions, enabling the creation of high-purity crystals that are free from inclusions or fractures.

Synthetic quartz is typically colorless and transparent, although colored varieties—such as amethyst, citrine, and smoky quartz—can be created through doping with trace elements or subsequent irradiation. Crystallizing in the hexagonal system, synthetic quartz exhibits the same physical properties as its natural counterpart, including a hardness of 7 and strong durability.

Due to its consistency, synthetic quartz is widely used in both the electronics industry and jewelry. It offers an affordable, flawless alternative to natural quartz varieties in gem applications. Its purity and stability make it popular for high-clarity carvings, faceted stones, and metaphysical tools where energy conduction is essential. Synthetic quartz combines technological precision with timeless gemstone appeal, bridging the gap between natural beauty and human innovation.

Photos © Tom Schultz

Synthetic Rutile

RI	2.616–2.903	**Critical Angle**	31.2°
Birefringence	0.287	**Cleavage**	Good
SG	4.2–4.3	**Heat sensitivity**	Yes
Color	Colorless, red, golden, brown	**Polish methods**	Aluminum Oxide and Diamond
Spectrum	None distinctive	**Hardness**	6–6.5

Synthetic rutile, or "Titania," is a laboratory-grown form of titanium dioxide (TiO_2) primarily produced through flame fusion methods since the 1940s. It was one of the earliest diamond simulants, boasting extraordinary dispersion and brilliance; however, its strong body color and double refraction easily distinguish it from diamond.

Crystallizing in the tetragonal system, synthetic rutile can be produced in a variety of colors—yellow, golden, brown, and even deep red—depending on growth conditions and impurities. Colorless synthetic rutile mimics the fire of diamonds better than any material of its time. However, its relatively low hardness (about 6 on the Mohs scale) makes it impractical for daily-wear jewelry.

Despite its limitations, synthetic rutile has played a pivotal role in the history of synthetic gemstones. It remains valued today for its exceptional sparkle, historical significance, and metaphysical association with vitality and creative energy. As a gemstone, synthetic rutile offers both dazzling optics and a nostalgic link to gemological innovation.

Rough gem © Tom Schulz, Cut gem © Victor Tuzlukov Somewhere In The Rainbow

Synthetic Spinel

RI	1.712–1.736	**Critical Angle**	41.4°
Birefringence	None (Isotropic)	**Cleavage**	None
SG	3.5–4.1	**Heat sensitivity**	No
Color	Red, blue, pink, violet	**Polish methods**	Aluminum Oxide and Diamond
Spectrum	Broad band around 460 nm	**Hardness**	7.5–8

Synthetic spinel, a magnesium aluminum oxide ($MgAl_2O_4$), is one of the earliest and most versatile laboratory-grown gemstones. It is primarily manufactured using the Verneuil flame fusion process, where powdered oxides are melted with an oxyhydrogen flame and then crystallized into flawless boule-shaped crystals. This rapid method allows for the mass production of synthetic spinel in a broad spectrum of colors.

Unlike natural spinel, synthetic varieties can be colorless or exhibit vivid shades of blue, pink, red, green, lavender, and black. They crystallize in the isometric system and demonstrate excellent durability, with a hardness of approximately 7.5–8 on the Mohs scale. Synthetic spinels often feature perfect clarity, vibrant color, and a vitreous luster; however, some show characteristic curved growth lines under magnification—a hallmark of flame fusion origin.

Affordable and durable, synthetic spinel has been widely used in class rings, birthstone jewelry, and costume pieces since the early 20th century. While natural spinel is now highly prized, synthetic spinel remains valued for its vibrant colors and toughness. It continues to symbolize energy, vitality, and resilience in metaphysical traditions. As a gemstone, synthetic spinel offers beauty, variety, and accessible luxury shaped by human craftsmanship.

Strontium Titanate

RI	2.410–2.540	**Critical Angle**	28.6°
Birefringence	None (Isotropic)	**Cleavage**	Perfect in 1 direction
SG	5.1	**Heat sensitivity**	Yes
Color	Colorless, yellowish	**Polish methods**	Aluminum Oxide and Diamond
Spectrum	None distinctive	**Hardness**	5.5

Strontium titanate ($SrTiO_3$) is a synthetic gemstone that was first developed in the 1950s as an early diamond simulant. It is produced through the flame fusion process, where powdered strontium and titanium oxides are melted under a high-temperature flame and crystallized into boule-shaped crystals.

Crystallizing in the isometric system, strontium titanate is typically colorless and exhibits remarkably high dispersion—meaning its "fire" (rainbow flashes) exceeds even that of diamond. However, its relative softness, with a Mohs hardness around 5.5–6, makes it unsuitable for rings or jewelry subject to heavy wear.

Strontium titanate's intense brilliance and affordable production costs made it popular for jewelry in the mid-20th century, before harder materials like cubic zirconia and moissanite gained prominence. Today, vintage strontium titanate gems are collector's items, celebrated for their breathtaking optical display and historic role in gemology.

Photo © Clemens Schwarzinger

Yttrium Aluminum Garnet (YAG)

RI	1.830–1.835	**Critical Angle**	32°
Birefringence	None (Isotropic)	**Cleavage**	None
SG	4.55–4.65	**Heat sensitivity**	No
Color	Colorless, yellow, green, red	**Polish methods**	Diamond
Spectrum	None distinctive	**Hardness**	8.5

Yttrium aluminum garnet (YAG, $Y_3Al_5O_{12}$) is a synthetic gemstone first developed in the 1960s as a diamond simulant, prior to the entry of cubic zirconia into the market. YAG is produced using the Czochralski pulling method, in which molten material crystallizes around a seed crystal to grow large, high-purity single crystals.

YAG crystallizes in the isometric system and can be produced in various colors, including colorless, green, blue, red, yellow, and orange, by incorporating trace elements during the growth process. It has a hardness of about 8.25 on the Mohs scale and exhibits strong brilliance with a high refractive index and moderate dispersion.

Though YAG has mainly been replaced by cubic zirconia for diamond simulation, it remains valued in jewelry for its durability and color versatility. It is also extensively used in lasers and other industrial applications. Symbolically, YAG represents innovation, strength, and precision—qualities reflected in both its gemological properties and its technological importance.

Rough gem: © Toms Box of Rocks, Cut gem: © Gems of Science

Gem Species Alphabetically

Gem Species	Refractive index	Birefringence	Critical Angle	Specifc Gravity	Hard-ness
Natural					
Agate (Moss Agate)	1.530–1.540	0.004	41.5	2.60–2.64	6.5–7
Andalusite	1.629–1.650	0.010–0.013	37.6°	3.1–3.2	7.5
Apatite	1.632–1.654	0.002–0.008	37.7°	3.1–3.2	5
Axinite	1.675–1.704	0.010–0.018	36.1°	3.2–3.3	6.5–7
Benitoite	1.756–1.804	0.048	34.2°	3.6–3.7	6.5
Beryl (Aquamarine, Morganite, Helidor, Emerald)	1.564–1.600	0.005–0.009	39.3°	2.6–2.9	7.5–8
Chrysoberyl	1.746–1.755	0.008–0.010	35°	3.7–3.8	8.5
Clinozoisite (Epidote Group)	1.725–1.768	0.036–0.048	36°	3.3–3.5	6–7
Confetti Sunstone (Feldspar)	1.537–1.547	.007–.010	41.3	2.65–2.70	6–6.5
Corundum (Sapphire, Ruby)	1.762–1.770	0.008	34.4°	3.9–4.1	9
Cuprite	2.849–2.951	None (Isotropic)	20.3°	6.1	3.5–4
Danburite	1.627–1.636	0.009	37.9°	3	7–7.5
Diamond	2.417	None (Isotropic)	24.4°	3.52	10
Diopside	1.663–1.701	0.038	36.5°	3.2–3.4	5.5–6.5
Epidote Group	1.725–1.768	0.043	34.9°	3.3–3.5	6–7
Feldspars	1.518–1.575	0.007–0.010	41°	2.5–2.7	6–6.5
Fluorite	1.434	None (Isotropic)	44.3°	3.0–3.2	4
Garnet	1.730–1.890	None (Isotropic)	43.5°	3.1–4.3	6.5–7.5
Idocrase	1.698–1.723	0.025	35.6°	3.3–3.5	6.5
Iolite (Cordierite)	1.55	0.017	40	2.6	7–7.5
Kornerupine	1.660–1.703	.036–.037	39.5	3.26–3.35	6.5–7
Kyanite	1.710–1.734	0.024	35.5°	3.6–3.7	4.5–7
Moldavite	1.480–1.510	None (Amophous)	42°	2.32–2.38	5.5

Gem Species	Refractive index	Birefringence	Critical Angle	Specifc Gravity	Hard-ness
Moonstone (Feldspar)	1.520–1.525	.005–.008	41.6	2.56–2.59	6–6.5
Obsidian	1.450–1.550	None (Amophous)	42.9°	2.3–2.6	5–5.5
Opal	1.370–1.470	None (Amophous)	43.2°	1.98–2.25	5.5–6.5
Opal–Fire Opal	1.370–1.470	None (Amophous)	43.2°	1.98–2.25	5.5–6.5
Oregon Sunstone (Feldspar)	1.560–1.572	.008–.010	40.9	2.62–2.68	6–6.5
Pearl	1.530–1.685			2.60–4.5	2.5–4.5
Peridot	1.650–1.703	0.035–0.038	36.7°	3.2–3.4	6.5–7
Phenacite	1.650–1.670	0.02	37°	2.9–3.0	7.5–8
Prehnite	1.610–1.669	0.059	38.2°	2.9–3.0	6–6.5
Quartz (Amethyst, Citrine, Smokey, Ametrine)	1.544–1.553	0.009	40.5°	2.65	7
Rhodochrosite	1.600–1.820	0.22	37.0°	3.5–3.7	3.5–4
Rutile	2.616–2.903	0.287	31.2°	4.2–4.3	6–6.5
Scapolite	1.540–1.579	0.006–0.020	40°	2.5–2.8	5.5–6
Sphalerite	2.368–2.371	0.003	25.3°	3.9 – 4.2	3.5 – 4
Sphene	1.843–2.110	0.267	32.5°	3.5 – 3.6	5 – 5.5
Spinel	1.712–1.736	None (Isotropic)	41.4°	3.5–4.1	7.5–8
Spodumene	1.648–1.680	0.014–0.016	36.8°	3.1–3.2	6.5–7
Sulfur	1.957–2.245	0.288	30.8	2.0–2.1	1.5–2.5
Tanzanite	1.685–1.707	0.008–0.013	40.5	3.35	7
Topaz	1.609–1.643	0.014	38.2°	3.4–3.6	8
Tourmaline	1.614–1.666	0.018–0.040	37.7°	3.0–3.3	7–7.5
Zincite	2.013–2.029	0.016	37.3°	5.7–6.4	4
Zircon - blue	1.810–2.024	0.059–0.078	38.9°	3.9–4.8	6–7.5

Gem Species Alphabetically

Gem Species	Refractive index	Birefringence	Critical Angle	Specifc Gravity	Hard-ness
Synthetics					
Alexandrite (color change Chryso-beryl)	1.746–1.755	0.008–0.010	37.6°	3.7–3.8	8.5
Aquamarine	1.577–1.583	0.005	39.3°	2.68–2.80	7.5–8
Corundum	1.762–1.770	0.008	34.4°	3.9–4.1	9
Cubic Zirconia	2.150–2.180	None (Isotropic)	28.5°	5.5–6.0	8–8.5
Emerald (Hydrothermal or Flux-Grown)	1.565–1.602	0.006–0.009	41.1°	2.68–2.78	7.5–8
Gadolinium Gallium Garnet (GGG)	1.950–1.970	None (Isotropic)	31.2°	7.05	6.5–7
Glass (including x-cube)	1.45–1.70	None	42-47	2.2–4.6	6
Lutetium Aluminum Garnet (LuAG)	1.83		32.3	6.7	8.5
Moissanite (Silicon Carbide)	2.648–2.691	0.043	24.5°	3.2	9.25
Opal	1.370–1.470	None (Amophous)	43.2°	1.98–2.25	5.5–6.5
Quartz rough	1.544–1.553	0.009	40.5°	2.65	7
Rutile rough	2.616 – 2.903	0.287	31.2°	4.2–4.3	6–6.5
Spinel	1.712–1.736	None (Isotropic)	41.4°	3.5–4.1	7.5–8
Strontium Titanate	2.410–2.540	None (Isotropic)	28.6°	5.1	5.5
Yttrium Aluminum Garnet (YAG)	1.830–1.835	None (Isotropic)	32.0°	4.55–4.65	8.5

Gem Species By Refractive Index

Gem Species	Refractive index	Birefringence	Critical Angle	Specifc Gravity	Hard-ness
Natural					
Fluorite	1.434	None (Isotropic)	44.3°	3.0–3.2	4
Opal	1.370–1.470	None (Isotropic)	43.2°	1.98–2.25	5.5–6.5
Opal–Fire Opal	1.370–1.470	None (Amophous)	43.2°	1.98–2.25	5.5–6.5
Obsidian	1.450–1.550	None (Amophous)	42.9°	2.3–2.6	5–5.5
Moldavite	1.480–1.510	None (Amophous)	42°	2.32–2.38	5.5
Feldspars	1.518–1.575	0.007–0.010	41°	2.5–2.7	6–6.5
Moonstone (Feldspar)	1.520–1.525	.005–.008	41.6	2.56–2.59	6–6.5
Agate (Moss Agate)	1.530–1.540	0.004	41.5	2.60–2.64	6.5–7
Pearl	1.530-1.685			2.60–4.5	2.5–4.5
Confetti Sunstone (Feldspar)	1.537–1.547	.007–.010	41.3	2.65–2.70	6–6.5
Scapolite	1.540–1.579	0.006–0.020	40°	2.5–2.8	5.5–6
Quartz (Amethyst, Citrine, Smokey, Ametrine)	1.544–1.553	0.009	40.5°	2.65	7
Iolite (Cordierite)	1.55	0.017	40	2.6	7–7.5
Oregon Sunstone (Feldspar)	1.560–1.572	.008–.010	40.9	2.62–2.68	6-6.5
Beryl (Aquamarine, Morganite, Helidor, Emerald)	1.564–1.600	0.005–0.009	39.3°	2.6–2.9	7.5–8
Rhodochrosite	1.600–1.820	0.22	37.0°	3.5–3.7	3.5–4
Topaz	1.609–1.643	0.014	38.2°	3.4–3.6	8
Prehnite	1.610–1.669	0.059	38.2°	2.9–3.0	6–6.5
Tourmaline	1.614–1.666	0.018–0.040	37.7°	3.0–3.3	7–7.5
Danburite	1.627–1.636	0.009	37.9°	3	7–7.5
Andalusite	1.629–1.650	0.010–0.013	37.6°	3.1–3.2	7.5
Apatite	1.632–1.654	0.002–0.008	37.7°	3.1–3.2	5

Gem Species By Refractive Index

Gem Species	Refractive index	Birefringence	Critical Angle	Specifc Gravity	Hard-ness
Spodumene	1.648–1.680	0.014–0.016	36.8°	3.1–3.2	6.5–7
Phenacite	1.650–1.670	0.02	37°	2.9–3.0	7.5–8
Peridot	1.650–1.703	0.035–0.038	36.7°	3.2–3.4	6.5–7
Kornerupine	1.660–1.703	.036–.037	39.5	3.26–3.35	6.5-7
Diopside	1.663–1.701	0.038	36.5°	3.2–3.4	5.5–6.5
Axinite	1.675–1.704	0.010–0.018	36.1°	3.2–3.3	6.5–7
Tanzanite	1.685–1.707	0.008–0.013	40.5	3.35	7
Idocrase	1.698–1.723	0.025	35.6°	3.3 – 3.5	6.5
Kyanite	1.710–1.734	0.024	35.5°	3.6–3.7	4.5–7
Spinel	1.712–1.736	None (Isotropic)	41.4°	3.5–4.1	7.5–8
Clinozoisite (Epidote Group)	1.725–1.768	0.036–0.048	36°	3.3–3.5	6–7
Epidote Group	1.725–1.768	0.043	34.9°	3.3–3.5	6–7
Garnet	1.730–1.890	None (Isotropic)	43.5°	3.1–4.3	6.5–7.5
Chrysoberyl	1.746–1.755	0.008–0.010	35°	3.7–3.8	8.5
Benitoite	1.756–1.804	0.048	34.2°	3.6–3.7	6.5
Corundum (Sapphire, Ruby)	1.762–1.770	0.008	34.4°	3.9–4.1	9
Zircon - blue	1.810–2.024	0.059–0.078	38.9°	3.9–4.8	6–7.5
Sphene	1.843–2.110	0.267	32.5°	3.5–3.6	5–5.5
Sulfur	1.957–2.245	0.288	30.8	2.0–2.1	1.5–2.5
Zincite	2.013–2.029	0.016	37.3°	5.7–6.4	4
Sphalerite	2.368–2.371	0.003	25.3°	3.9–4.2	3.5–4
Diamond	2.417	None (Isotropic)	24.4°	3.52	10
Rutile	2.616–2.903	0.287	31.2°	4.2–4.3	6–6.5
Cuprite	2.849–2.951	None (Isotropic)	20.3°	6.1	3.5–4

Gem Species By Refractive Index

Gem Species	Refractive index	Birefringence	Critical Angle	Specifc Gravity	Hard-ness
Synthetics					
Aquamarine	1.577–1.583	0.005	39.3°	2.68–2.80	7.5–8
Opal	1.370–1.470	None (Amophous)	43.2°	1.98–2.25	5.5–6.5
Glass (including x-cube)	1.45–1.70	None	42-47	2.2–4.6	6
Quartz rough	1.544–1.553	0.009	40.5°	2.65	7
Emerald (Hydrothermal or Flux-Grown)	1.565–1.602	0.006–0.009	41.1°	2.68–2.78	7.5–8
Spinel	1.712–1.736	None (Isotropic)	41.4°	3.5–4.1	7.5–8
Alexandrite (color change Chryso-beryl)	1.746–1.755	0.008–0.010	37.6°	3.7–3.8	8.5
Corundum	1.762–1.770	0.008	34.4°	3.9–4.1	9
Lutetium Aluminum Garnet (LuAG)	1.83		32.3	6.7	8.5
Yttrium Aluminum Garnet (YAG)	1.830–1.835	None (Isotropic)	32.0°	4.55–4.65	8.5
Gadolinium Galli-um Garnet (GGG)	1.950–1.970	None (Isotropic)	31.2°	7.05	6.5–7
Cubic Zirconia	2.150–2.180	None (Isotropic)	28.5°	5.5–6.0	8–8.5
Strontium Titanate	2.410–2.540	None (Isotropic)	28.6°	5.1	5.5
Rutile rough	2.616–2.903	0.287	31.2°	4.2–4.3	6–6.5
Moissanite (Silicon Carbide)	2.648–2.691	0.043	24.5°	3.2	9.25

Gem Species By Specific Gravity

Gem Species	Refractive index	Birefringence	Critical Angle	Specifc Gravity	Hard-ness
Natural					
Opal	1.370–1.470	None (Amorphous)	43.2°	1.98–2.25	5.5–6.5
Opal–Fire Opal	1.370–1.470	None (Amorphous)	43.2°	1.98–2.25	5.5–6.5
Sulfur	1.957–2.245	0.288	30.8	2.0–2.1	1.5–2.5
Obsidian	1.450–1.550	None (Amorphous)	42.9°	2.3–2.6	5–5.5
Moldavite	1.480–1.510	None (Amorphous)	42°	2.32–2.38	5.5
Feldspars	1.518–1.575	0.007–0.010	41°	2.5–2.7	6–6.5
Scapolite	1.540–1.579	0.006–0.020	40°	2.5–2.8	5.5–6
Moonstone (Feldspar)	1.520–1.525	.005–.008	41.6	2.56–2.59	6–6.5
Iolite (Cordierite)	1.55	0.017	40	2.6	7–7.5
Quartz (Amethyst, Citrine, Smokey, Ametrine)	1.544–1.553	0.009	40.5°	2.65	7
Beryl (Aquamarine, Morganite, Helidor, Emerald)	1.564–1.600	0.005–0.009	39.3°	2.6–2.9	7.5–8
Agate (Moss Agate)	1.530–1.540	0.004	41.5	2.60–2.64	6.5-7
Pearl	1.530–1.685			2.60–4.5	2.5–4.5
Oregon Sunstone (Feldspar)	1.560–1.572	.008–.010	40.9	2.62–2.68	6–6.5
Confetti Sunstone (Feldspar)	1.537–1.547	.007–.010	41.3	2.65–2.70	6–6.5
Phenacite	1.650–1.670	0.02	37°	2.9–3.0	7.5–8
Prehnite	1.610–1.669	0.059	38.2°	2.9–3.0	6–6.5
Danburite	1.627–1.636	0.009	37.9°	3	7–7.5
Fluorite	1.434	None (Isotropic)	44.3°	3.0–3.2	4
Tourmaline	1.614–1.666	0.018–0.040	37.7°	3.0–3.3	7–7.5
Andalusite	1.629–1.650	0.010–0.013	37.6°	3.1–3.2	7.5
Apatite	1.632–1.654	0.002–0.008	37.7°	3.1–3.2	5

Gem Species By Specific Gravity

Gem Species	Refractive index	Birefringence	Critical Angle	Specifc Gravity	Hard-ness
Spodumene	1.648–1.680	0.014–0.016	36.8°	3.1–3.2	6.5–7
Garnet	1.730–1.890	None (Isotropic)	43.5°	3.1–4.3	6.5–7.5
Axinite	1.675–1.704	0.010–0.018	36.1°	3.2–3.3	6.5–7
Diopside	1.663–1.701	0.038	36.5°	3.2–3.4	5.5–6.5
Peridot	1.650–1.703	0.035–0.038	36.7°	3.2–3.4	6.5–7
Kornerupine	1.660–1.703	.036–.037	39.5	3.26–3.35	6.5–7
Clinozoisite (Epidote Group)	1.725–1.768	0.036–0.048	36°	3.3–3.5	6–7
Epidote Group	1.725–1.768	0.043	36°	3.3–3.5	6–7
Idocrase	1.698–1.723	0.025	35.6°	3.3–3.5	6.5
Tanzanite	1.685–1.707	0.008–0.013	40.5	3.35	7
Topaz	1.609–1.643	0.014	38.2°	3.4–3.6	8
Sphene	1.843–2.110	0.267	32.5°	3.5–3.6	5–5.5
Rhodochrosite	1.600–1.820	0.22	37.0°	3.5–3.7	3.5–4
Diamond	2.417	None (Isotropic)	24.4°	3.52	10
Spinel	1.712–1.736	None (Isotropic)	41.4°	3.5–4.1	7.5–8
Benitoite	1.756–1.804	0.048	34.2°	3.6–3.7	6.5
Kyanite	1.710–1.734	0.024	35.5°	3.6–3.7	4.5 – 7
Chrysoberyl	1.746–1.755	0.008–0.010	35°	3.7–3.8	8.5
Corundum (Sapphire, Ruby)	1.762–1.770	0.008	34.4°	3.9–4.1	9
Sphalerite	2.368–2.371	0.003	25.3°	3.9–4.2	3.5–4
Zircon–blue	1.810–2.024	0.059–0.078	38.9°	3.9–4.8	6–7.5
Rutile	2.616–2.903	0.287	31.2°	4.2–4.3	6–6.5
Zincite	2.013–2.029	0.016	37.3°	5.7–6.4	4
Cuprite	2.849–2.951	None (Isotropic)	20.3°	6.1	3.5–4

Gem Species By Specific Gravity

Gem Species	Refractive index	Birefringence	Critical Angle	Specifc Gravity	Hard-ness
Synthetics					
Opal	1.370–1.470	None (Amorphous)	43.2°	1.98–2.25	5.5–6.5
Glass (including x-cube)	1.45–1.70	None	42–47	2.2–4.6	6
Quartz rough	1.544–1.553	0.009	40.5°	2.65	7
Emerald (Hydrothermal or Flux-Grown)	1.565–1.602	0.006–0.009	41.1°	2.68–2.78	7.5–8
Aquamarine	1.577–1.583	0.005	39.3°	2.68–2.80	7.5–8
Moissanite (Silicon Carbide)	2.648–2.691	0.043	24.5°	3.2	9.25
Spinel	1.712–1.736	None (Isotropic)	41.4°	3.5–4.1	7.5–8
Alexandrite (color change Chrysoberyl)	1.746–1.755	0.008–0.010	37.6°	3.7–3.8	8.5
Corundum	1.762–1.770	0.008	34.4°	3.9–4.1	9
Rutile rough	2.616–2.903	0.287	31.2°	4.2–4.3	6–6.5
Yttrium Aluminum Garnet (YAG)	1.830–1.835	None (Isotropic)	32.0°	4.55–4.65	8.5
Strontium Titanate	2.410–2.540	None (Isotropic)	28.6°	5.1	5.5
Cubic Zirconia	2.150–2.180	None (Isotropic)	28.5°	5.5–6.0	8–8.5
Lutetium Aluminum Garnet (LuAG)	1.83		32.3	6.7	8.5
Gadolinium Galli-um Garnet (GGG)	1.950–1.970	None (Isotropic)	31.2°	7.05	6.5–7

Journal Pages

Gem Cutting Log

Date		Reference #	
Gem Species		Source	
Starting Weight		Finish Weight	
Start Dimensions		Final Dimensions	
Design/Shape			

Pavillion

Angle	Indices

Crown

Angle	Indices

Gem Cutting Log

Date		Reference #	
Gem Species		Source	
Starting Weight		Finish Weight	
Start Dimensions		Final Dimensions	
Design/Shape			

Pavillion

Angle	Indices

Crown

Angle	Indices

Gem Cutting Log

Date		Reference #	
Gem Species		Source	
Starting Weight		Finish Weight	
Start Dimensions		Final Dimensions	
Design/Shape			

Pavillion

Angle	Indices

Crown

Angle	Indices

Gem Cutting Log

Date		Reference #	
Gem Species		Source	
Starting Weight		Finish Weight	
Start Dimensions		Final Dimensions	
Design/Shape			

Pavillion

Angle	Indices

Crown

Angle	Indices

Gem Cutting Log

Date		Reference #	
Gem Species		Source	
Starting Weight		Finish Weight	
Start Dimensions		Final Dimensions	
Design/Shape			

Pavillion

Angle	Indices

Crown

Angle	Indices

Gem Cutting Log

Date		Reference #	
Gem Species		Source	
Starting Weight		Finish Weight	
Start Dimensions		Final Dimensions	
Design/Shape			

Pavillion

Angle	Indices

Crown

Angle	Indices

Gem Cutting Log

Date		Reference #	
Gem Species		Source	
Starting Weight		Finish Weight	
Start Dimensions		Final Dimensions	
Design/Shape			

Pavillion

Angle	Indices

Crown

Angle	Indices

Gem Cutting Log

Date		Reference #	
Gem Species		Source	
Starting Weight		Finish Weight	
Start Dimensions		Final Dimensions	
Design/Shape			

Pavillion

Angle	Indices

Crown

Angle	Indices

Gem Cutting Log

Date		Reference #	
Gem Species		Source	
Starting Weight		Finish Weight	
Start Dimensions		Final Dimensions	
Design/Shape			

Pavillion

Angle	Indices

Crown

Angle	Indices

Gem Cutting Log

Date		Reference #	
Gem Species		Source	
Starting Weight		Finish Weight	
Start Dimensions		Final Dimensions	
Design/Shape			

Pavillion

Angle	Indices

Crown

Angle	Indices

Gem Cutting Log

Date		Reference #	
Gem Species		Source	
Starting Weight		Finish Weight	
Start Dimensions		Final Dimensions	
Design/Shape			

Pavillion

Angle	Indices

Crown

Angle	Indices

Date		Reference #	
Gem Species		Source	
Starting Weight		Finish Weight	
Start Dimensions		Final Dimensions	
Design/Shape			

Pavillion

Angle	Indices

Crown

Angle	Indices

Gem Cutting Log

Date		Reference #	
Gem Species		Source	
Starting Weight		Finish Weight	
Start Dimensions		Final Dimensions	
Design/Shape			

Pavillion

Angle	Indices

Crown

Angle	Indices

Gem Cutting Log

Date		Reference #	
Gem Species		Source	
Starting Weight		Finish Weight	
Start Dimensions		Final Dimensions	
Design/Shape			

Pavillion

Angle	Indices

Crown

Angle	Indices

Gem Cutting Log

Date		Reference #	
Gem Species		Source	
Starting Weight		Finish Weight	
Start Dimensions		Final Dimensions	
Design/Shape			

Pavillion

Angle	Indices

Crown

Angle	Indices

Gem Cutting Log

Date		Reference #	
Gem Species		Source	
Starting Weight		Finish Weight	
Start Dimensions		Final Dimensions	
Design/Shape			

Pavillion

Angle	Indices

Crown

Angle	Indices

Gem Cutting Log

Date		Reference #	
Gem Species		Source	
Starting Weight		Finish Weight	
Start Dimensions		Final Dimensions	
Design/Shape			

Pavillion

Angle	Indices

Crown

Angle	Indices

Gem Cutting Log

Date	
Gem Species	
Starting Weight	
Start Dimensions	
Design/Shape	

Reference #	
Source	
Finish Weight	
Final Dimensions	

Pavillion

Angle	Indices

Crown

Angle	Indices

Gem Cutting Log

Date		Reference #	
Gem Species		Source	
Starting Weight		Finish Weight	
Start Dimensions		Final Dimensions	
Design/Shape			

Pavillion

Angle	Indices

Crown

Angle	Indices

Gem Cutting Log

Date		Reference #	
Gem Species		Source	
Starting Weight		Finish Weight	
Start Dimensions		Final Dimensions	
Design/Shape			

Pavillion

Angle	Indices

Crown

Angle	Indices

Gem Cutting Log

Date		Reference #	
Gem Species		Source	
Starting Weight		Finish Weight	
Start Dimensions		Final Dimensions	
Design/Shape			

Pavillion

Angle	Indices

Crown

Angle	Indices

Gem Cutting Log

Date		Reference #	
Gem Species		Source	
Starting Weight		Finish Weight	
Start Dimensions		Final Dimensions	
Design/Shape			

Pavillion

Angle	Indices

Crown

Angle	Indices

Gem Cutting Log

Date		Reference #	
Gem Species		Source	
Starting Weight		Finish Weight	
Start Dimensions		Final Dimensions	
Design/Shape			

Pavillion

Angle	Indices

Crown

Angle	Indices

Date	
Gem Species	
Starting Weight	
Start Dimensions	
Design/Shape	

Reference #	
Source	
Finish Weight	
Final Dimensions	

Pavillion

Angle	Indices

Crown

Angle	Indices

Gem Cutting Log

Date		Reference #	
Gem Species		Source	
Starting Weight		Finish Weight	
Start Dimensions		Final Dimensions	
Design/Shape			

Pavillion

Angle	Indices

Crown

Angle	Indices

Date		Reference #	
Gem Species		Source	
Starting Weight		Finish Weight	
Start Dimensions		Final Dimensions	
Design/Shape			

Pavillion

Angle	Indices

Crown

Angle	Indices

Gem Cutting Log

Date		Reference #	
Gem Species		Source	
Starting Weight		Finish Weight	
Start Dimensions		Final Dimensions	
Design/Shape			

Pavillion

Angle	Indices

Crown

Angle	Indices

Gem Cutting Log

Date		Reference #	
Gem Species		Source	
Starting Weight		Finish Weight	
Start Dimensions		Final Dimensions	
Design/Shape			

Pavillion

Angle	Indices

Crown

Angle	Indices

Gem Cutting Log

Date		Reference #	
Gem Species		Source	
Starting Weight		Finish Weight	
Start Dimensions		Final Dimensions	
Design/Shape			

Pavillion

Angle	Indices

Crown

Angle	Indices

Date		Reference #	
Gem Species		Source	
Starting Weight		Finish Weight	
Start Dimensions		Final Dimensions	
Design/Shape			

Pavillion

Angle	Indices

Crown

Angle	Indices

Gem Cutting Log

Date		Reference #	
Gem Species		Source	
Starting Weight		Finish Weight	
Start Dimensions		Final Dimensions	
Design/Shape			

Pavillion

Angle	Indices

Crown

Angle	Indices

Gem Cutting Log

Date		**Reference #**	
Gem Species		**Source**	
Starting Weight		**Finish Weight**	
Start Dimensions		**Final Dimensions**	
Design/Shape			

Pavillion

Angle	Indices

Crown

Angle	Indices

Gem Cutting Log

Date		**Reference #**	
Gem Species		**Source**	
Starting Weight		**Finish Weight**	
Start Dimensions		**Final Dimensions**	
Design/Shape			

Pavillion

Angle	Indices

Crown

Angle	Indices

Gem Cutting Log

Date		Reference #	
Gem Species		Source	
Starting Weight		Finish Weight	
Start Dimensions		Final Dimensions	
Design/Shape			

Pavillion

Angle	Indices

Crown

Angle	Indices

Gem Cutting Log

Date		Reference #	
Gem Species		Source	
Starting Weight		Finish Weight	
Start Dimensions		Final Dimensions	
Design/Shape			

Pavillion

Angle	Indices

Crown

Angle	Indices

Gem Cutting Log

Date		Reference #	
Gem Species		Source	
Starting Weight		Finish Weight	
Start Dimensions		Final Dimensions	
Design/Shape			

Pavillion

Angle	Indices

Crown

Angle	Indices

Gem Cutting Log

Date		Reference #	
Gem Species		Source	
Starting Weight		Finish Weight	
Start Dimensions		Final Dimensions	
Design/Shape			

Pavillion

Angle	Indices

Crown

Angle	Indices

Gem Cutting Log

Date		Reference #	
Gem Species		Source	
Starting Weight		Finish Weight	
Start Dimensions		Final Dimensions	
Design/Shape			

Pavillion

Angle	Indices

Crown

Angle	Indices

Gem Cutting Log

Date		Reference #	
Gem Species		Source	
Starting Weight		Finish Weight	
Start Dimensions		Final Dimensions	
Design/Shape			

Pavillion

Angle	Indices

Crown

Angle	Indices

Date		Reference #	
Gem Species		Source	
Starting Weight		Finish Weight	
Start Dimensions		Final Dimensions	
Design/Shape			

Pavillion

Angle	Indices

Crown

Angle	Indices

Gem Cutting Log

Date		Reference #	
Gem Species		Source	
Starting Weight		Finish Weight	
Start Dimensions		Final Dimensions	
Design/Shape			

Pavillion

Angle	Indices

Crown

Angle	Indices

Date		Reference #	
Gem Species		Source	
Starting Weight		Finish Weight	
Start Dimensions		Final Dimensions	
Design/Shape			

Pavillion

Angle	Indices

Crown

Angle	Indices

Gem Cutting Log

Date		Reference #	
Gem Species		Source	
Starting Weight		Finish Weight	
Start Dimensions		Final Dimensions	
Design/Shape			

Pavillion

Angle	Indices

Crown

Angle	Indices

Gem Cutting Log

Date		Reference #	
Gem Species		Source	
Starting Weight		Finish Weight	
Start Dimensions		Final Dimensions	
Design/Shape			

Pavillion

Angle	Indices

Crown

Angle	Indices

Gem Cutting Log

Date		Reference #	
Gem Species		Source	
Starting Weight		Finish Weight	
Start Dimensions		Final Dimensions	
Design/Shape			

Pavillion

Angle	Indices

Crown

Angle	Indices

Date	
Gem Species	
Starting Weight	
Start Dimensions	
Design/Shape	

Reference #	
Source	
Finish Weight	
Final Dimensions	

Pavillion

Angle	Indices

Crown

Angle	Indices

Gem Cutting Log

Date		Reference #	
Gem Species		Source	
Starting Weight		Finish Weight	
Start Dimensions		Final Dimensions	
Design/Shape			

Pavillion

Angle	Indices

Crown

Angle	Indices

Date		Reference #	
Gem Species		Source	
Starting Weight		Finish Weight	
Start Dimensions		Final Dimensions	
Design/Shape			

Pavillion

Angle	Indices

Crown

Angle	Indices

Gem Cutting Log

Date		Reference #	
Gem Species		Source	
Starting Weight		Finish Weight	
Start Dimensions		Final Dimensions	
Design/Shape			

Pavillion

Angle	Indices

Crown

Angle	Indices

Gem Cutting Log

Date		Reference #	
Gem Species		Source	
Starting Weight		Finish Weight	
Start Dimensions		Final Dimensions	
Design/Shape			

Pavillion

Angle	Indices

Crown

Angle	Indices

Gem Cutting Log

Date		Reference #	
Gem Species		Source	
Starting Weight		Finish Weight	
Start Dimensions		Final Dimensions	
Design/Shape			

Pavillion

Angle	Indices

Crown

Angle	Indices

Gem Cutting Log

Date		**Reference #**	
Gem Species		**Source**	
Starting Weight		**Finish Weight**	
Start Dimensions		**Final Dimensions**	
Design/Shape			

Pavillion

Angle	Indices

Crown

Angle	Indices

Gem Cutting Log

Date		**Reference #**	
Gem Species		**Source**	
Starting Weight		**Finish Weight**	
Start Dimensions		**Final Dimensions**	
Design/Shape			

Pavillion

Angle	Indices

Crown

Angle	Indices

Gem Cutting Log

Date		Reference #	
Gem Species		Source	
Starting Weight		Finish Weight	
Start Dimensions		Final Dimensions	
Design/Shape			

Pavillion

Angle	Indices

Crown

Angle	Indices

Gem Cutting Log

Date		Reference #	
Gem Species		Source	
Starting Weight		Finish Weight	
Start Dimensions		Final Dimensions	
Design/Shape			

Pavillion

Angle	Indices

Crown

Angle	Indices

Gem Cutting Log

Date		**Reference #**	
Gem Species		**Source**	
Starting Weight		**Finish Weight**	
Start Dimensions		**Final Dimensions**	
Design/Shape			

Pavillion

Angle	Indices

Crown

Angle	Indices

Gem Cutting Log

Date		Reference #	
Gem Species		Source	
Starting Weight		Finish Weight	
Start Dimensions		Final Dimensions	
Design/Shape			

Pavillion

Angle	Indices

Crown

Angle	Indices

Date		Reference #	
Gem Species		Source	
Starting Weight		Finish Weight	
Start Dimensions		Final Dimensions	
Design/Shape			

Pavillion

Angle	Indices

Crown

Angle	Indices

Gem Cutting Log

Date		Reference #	
Gem Species		Source	
Starting Weight		Finish Weight	
Start Dimensions		Final Dimensions	
Design/Shape			

Pavillion

Angle	Indices

Crown

Angle	Indices

Gem Cutting Log

Date		Reference #	
Gem Species		Source	
Starting Weight		Finish Weight	
Start Dimensions		Final Dimensions	
Design/Shape			

Pavillion

Angle	Indices

Crown

Angle	Indices

Gem Cutting Log

Date		**Reference #**	
Gem Species		**Source**	
Starting Weight		**Finish Weight**	
Start Dimensions		**Final Dimensions**	
Design/Shape			

Pavillion

Angle	Indices

Crown

Angle	Indices

Date		Reference #	
Gem Species		Source	
Starting Weight		Finish Weight	
Start Dimensions		Final Dimensions	
Design/Shape			

Pavillion

Angle	Indices

Crown

Angle	Indices

Gem Cutting Log

Date		Reference #	
Gem Species		Source	
Starting Weight		Finish Weight	
Start Dimensions		Final Dimensions	
Design/Shape			

Pavillion

Angle	Indices

Crown

Angle	Indices

Gem Cutting Log

Date		Reference #	
Gem Species		Source	
Starting Weight		Finish Weight	
Start Dimensions		Final Dimensions	
Design/Shape			

Pavillion

Angle	Indices

Crown

Angle	Indices

Gem Cutting Log

Date	
Gem Species	
Starting Weight	
Start Dimensions	
Design/Shape	

Reference #	
Source	
Finish Weight	
Final Dimensions	

Pavillion

Angle	Indices

Crown

Angle	Indices

Gem Cutting Log

Date		Reference #	
Gem Species		Source	
Starting Weight		Finish Weight	
Start Dimensions		Final Dimensions	
Design/Shape			

Pavillion

Angle	Indices

Crown

Angle	Indices

Gem Cutting Log

Date		Reference #	
Gem Species		Source	
Starting Weight		Finish Weight	
Start Dimensions		Final Dimensions	
Design/Shape			

Pavillion

Angle	Indices

Crown

Angle	Indices

Gem Cutting Log

Date	
Gem Species	
Starting Weight	
Start Dimensions	
Design/Shape	

Reference #	
Source	
Finish Weight	
Final Dimensions	

Pavillion

Angle	Indices

Crown

Angle	Indices

Gem Cutting Log

Date	
Gem Species	
Starting Weight	
Start Dimensions	
Design/Shape	

Reference #	
Source	
Finish Weight	
Final Dimensions	

Pavillion

Angle	Indices

Crown

Angle	Indices

Gem Cutting Log

Date		Reference #	
Gem Species		Source	
Starting Weight		Finish Weight	
Start Dimensions		Final Dimensions	
Design/Shape			

Pavillion

Angle	Indices

Crown

Angle	Indices

Gem Cutting Log

Date		Reference #	
Gem Species		Source	
Starting Weight		Finish Weight	
Start Dimensions		Final Dimensions	
Design/Shape			

Pavillion

Angle	Indices

Crown

Angle	Indices

Gem Cutting Log

Date	
Gem Species	
Starting Weight	
Start Dimensions	
Design/Shape	

Reference #	
Source	
Finish Weight	
Final Dimensions	

Pavillion

Angle	Indices

Crown

Angle	Indices

Rough Catalog

Date		Gem Species	
Purchased From		$ per	____ct ____gm
Number Pieces		Total Cost	
Total Weight		Reference #	
Notes			

Date		Gem Species	
Purchased From		$ per	____ct ____gm
Number Pieces		Total Cost	
Total Weight		Reference #	
Notes			

Date		Gem Species	
Purchased From		$ per	____ct ____gm
Number Pieces		Total Cost	
Total Weight		Reference #	
Notes			

Date		Gem Species	
Purchased From		$ per	____ct ____gm
Number Pieces		Total Cost	
Total Weight		Reference #	
Notes			

Date		Gem Species	
Purchased From		$ per	____ct ____gm
Number Pieces		Total Cost	
Total Weight		Reference #	
Notes			

Date
Purchased From
Number Pieces
Total Weight
Notes

Gem Species
$ per ____ct ____gm
Total Cost
Reference #

Date
Purchased From
Number Pieces
Total Weight
Notes

Gem Species
$ per ____ct ____gm
Total Cost
Reference #

Date
Purchased From
Number Pieces
Total Weight
Notes

Gem Species
$ per ____ct ____gm
Total Cost
Reference #

Date
Purchased From
Number Pieces
Total Weight
Notes

Gem Species
$ per ____ct ____gm
Total Cost
Reference #

Date
Purchased From
Number Pieces
Total Weight
Notes

Gem Species
$ per ____ct ____gm
Total Cost
Reference #

Rough Catalog

Date		**Gem Species**	
Purchased From		**$ per**	_____ct _____gm
Number Pieces		**Total Cost**	
Total Weight		**Reference #**	
Notes			

Date		**Gem Species**	
Purchased From		**$ per**	_____ct _____gm
Number Pieces		**Total Cost**	
Total Weight		**Reference #**	
Notes			

Date		**Gem Species**	
Purchased From		**$ per**	_____ct _____gm
Number Pieces		**Total Cost**	
Total Weight		**Reference #**	
Notes			

Date		**Gem Species**	
Purchased From		**$ per**	_____ct _____gm
Number Pieces		**Total Cost**	
Total Weight		**Reference #**	
Notes			

Date		**Gem Species**	
Purchased From		**$ per**	_____ct _____gm
Number Pieces		**Total Cost**	
Total Weight		**Reference #**	
Notes			

Date		Gem Species	
Purchased From		$ per	____ct ____gm
Number Pieces		Total Cost	
Total Weight		Reference #	
Notes			

Date		Gem Species	
Purchased From		$ per	____ct ____gm
Number Pieces		Total Cost	
Total Weight		Reference #	
Notes			

Date		Gem Species	
Purchased From		$ per	____ct ____gm
Number Pieces		Total Cost	
Total Weight		Reference #	
Notes			

Date		Gem Species	
Purchased From		$ per	____ct ____gm
Number Pieces		Total Cost	
Total Weight		Reference #	
Notes			

Date		Gem Species	
Purchased From		$ per	____ct ____gm
Number Pieces		Total Cost	
Total Weight		Reference #	
Notes			

Rough Catalog

Date		Gem Species	
Purchased From		$ per	____ct ____gm
Number Pieces		Total Cost	
Total Weight		Reference #	
Notes			

Date		Gem Species	
Purchased From		$ per	____ct ____gm
Number Pieces		Total Cost	
Total Weight		Reference #	
Notes			

Date		Gem Species	
Purchased From		$ per	____ct ____gm
Number Pieces		Total Cost	
Total Weight		Reference #	
Notes			

Date		Gem Species	
Purchased From		$ per	____ct ____gm
Number Pieces		Total Cost	
Total Weight		Reference #	
Notes			

Date		Gem Species	
Purchased From		$ per	____ct ____gm
Number Pieces		Total Cost	
Total Weight		Reference #	
Notes			

Date		**Gem Species**	
Purchased From		**$ per**	____ct ____gm
Number Pieces		**Total Cost**	
Total Weight		**Reference #**	
Notes			

Date		**Gem Species**	
Purchased From		**$ per**	____ct ____gm
Number Pieces		**Total Cost**	
Total Weight		**Reference #**	
Notes			

Date		**Gem Species**	
Purchased From		**$ per**	____ct ____gm
Number Pieces		**Total Cost**	
Total Weight		**Reference #**	
Notes			

Date		**Gem Species**	
Purchased From		**$ per**	____ct ____gm
Number Pieces		**Total Cost**	
Total Weight		**Reference #**	
Notes			

Date		**Gem Species**	
Purchased From		**$ per**	____ct ____gm
Number Pieces		**Total Cost**	
Total Weight		**Reference #**	
Notes			

Rough Catalog

Date | Gem Species
Purchased From | $ per ____ct ____gm
Number Pieces | Total Cost
Total Weight | Reference #
Notes

Date | Gem Species
Purchased From | $ per ____ct ____gm
Number Pieces | Total Cost
Total Weight | Reference #
Notes

Date | Gem Species
Purchased From | $ per ____ct ____gm
Number Pieces | Total Cost
Total Weight | Reference #
Notes

Date | Gem Species
Purchased From | $ per ____ct ____gm
Number Pieces | Total Cost
Total Weight | Reference #
Notes

Date | Gem Species
Purchased From | $ per ____ct ____gm
Number Pieces | Total Cost
Total Weight | Reference #
Notes

Date
Purchased From
Number Pieces
Total Weight
Notes
Gem Species
$ per ____ct ____gm
Total Cost
Reference #

Date
Purchased From
Number Pieces
Total Weight
Notes
Gem Species
$ per ____ct ____gm
Total Cost
Reference #

Date
Purchased From
Number Pieces
Total Weight
Notes
Gem Species
$ per ____ct ____gm
Total Cost
Reference #

Date
Purchased From
Number Pieces
Total Weight
Notes
Gem Species
$ per ____ct ____gm
Total Cost
Reference #

Date
Purchased From
Number Pieces
Total Weight
Notes
Gem Species
$ per ____ct ____gm
Total Cost
Reference #

Rough Catalog

Date
Purchased From
Number Pieces
Total Weight
Notes

Gem Species
$ per ____ ct ____ gm
Total Cost
Reference #

Date
Purchased From
Number Pieces
Total Weight
Notes

Gem Species
$ per ____ ct ____ gm
Total Cost
Reference #

Date
Purchased From
Number Pieces
Total Weight
Notes

Gem Species
$ per ____ ct ____ gm
Total Cost
Reference #

Date
Purchased From
Number Pieces
Total Weight
Notes

Gem Species
$ per ____ ct ____ gm
Total Cost
Reference #

Date
Purchased From
Number Pieces
Total Weight
Notes

Gem Species
$ per ____ ct ____ gm
Total Cost
Reference #

Date		Gem Species	
Purchased From		$ per	____ct ____gm
Number Pieces		Total Cost	
Total Weight		Reference #	
Notes			

Date		Gem Species	
Purchased From		$ per	____ct ____gm
Number Pieces		Total Cost	
Total Weight		Reference #	
Notes			

Date		Gem Species	
Purchased From		$ per	____ct ____gm
Number Pieces		Total Cost	
Total Weight		Reference #	
Notes			

Date		Gem Species	
Purchased From		$ per	____ct ____gm
Number Pieces		Total Cost	
Total Weight		Reference #	
Notes			

Date		Gem Species	
Purchased From		$ per	____ct ____gm
Number Pieces		Total Cost	
Total Weight		Reference #	
Notes			

Date
Purchased From
Number Pieces
Total Weight
Notes

Gem Species
$ per ____ct ____gm
Total Cost
Reference #

Date
Purchased From
Number Pieces
Total Weight
Notes

Gem Species
$ per ____ct ____gm
Total Cost
Reference #

Date
Purchased From
Number Pieces
Total Weight
Notes

Gem Species
$ per ____ct ____gm
Total Cost
Reference #

Date
Purchased From
Number Pieces
Total Weight
Notes

Gem Species
$ per ____ct ____gm
Total Cost
Reference #

Date
Purchased From
Number Pieces
Total Weight
Notes

Gem Species
$ per ____ct ____gm
Total Cost
Reference #

Date
Purchased From
Number Pieces
Total Weight
Notes

Gem Species
$ per ____ct ____gm
Total Cost
Reference #

Date
Purchased From
Number Pieces
Total Weight
Notes

Gem Species
$ per ____ct ____gm
Total Cost
Reference #

Date
Purchased From
Number Pieces
Total Weight
Notes

Gem Species
$ per ____ct ____gm
Total Cost
Reference #

Date
Purchased From
Number Pieces
Total Weight
Notes

Gem Species
$ per ____ct ____gm
Total Cost
Reference #

Date
Purchased From
Number Pieces
Total Weight
Notes

Gem Species
$ per ____ct ____gm
Total Cost
Reference #

Rough Catalog

Date
Purchased From
Number Pieces
Total Weight
Notes

Gem Species
$ per ____ct ____gm
Total Cost
Reference #

Date
Purchased From
Number Pieces
Total Weight
Notes

Gem Species
$ per ____ct ____gm
Total Cost
Reference #

Date
Purchased From
Number Pieces
Total Weight
Notes

Gem Species
$ per ____ct ____gm
Total Cost
Reference #

Date
Purchased From
Number Pieces
Total Weight
Notes

Gem Species
$ per ____ct ____gm
Total Cost
Reference #

Date
Purchased From
Number Pieces
Total Weight
Notes

Gem Species
$ per ____ct ____gm
Total Cost
Reference #

Date		Gem Species	
Purchased From		$ per	____ct ____gm
Number Pieces		Total Cost	
Total Weight		Reference #	
Notes			

Date		Gem Species	
Purchased From		$ per	____ct ____gm
Number Pieces		Total Cost	
Total Weight		Reference #	
Notes			

Date		Gem Species	
Purchased From		$ per	____ct ____gm
Number Pieces		Total Cost	
Total Weight		Reference #	
Notes			

Date		Gem Species	
Purchased From		$ per	____ct ____gm
Number Pieces		Total Cost	
Total Weight		Reference #	
Notes			

Date		Gem Species	
Purchased From		$ per	____ct ____gm
Number Pieces		Total Cost	
Total Weight		Reference #	
Notes			

Rough Catalog

Date		Gem Species	
Purchased From		$ per	____ct ____gm
Number Pieces		Total Cost	
Total Weight		Reference #	
Notes			

Date		Gem Species	
Purchased From		$ per	____ct ____gm
Number Pieces		Total Cost	
Total Weight		Reference #	
Notes			

Date		Gem Species	
Purchased From		$ per	____ct ____gm
Number Pieces		Total Cost	
Total Weight		Reference #	
Notes			

Date		Gem Species	
Purchased From		$ per	____ct ____gm
Number Pieces		Total Cost	
Total Weight		Reference #	
Notes			

Date		Gem Species	
Purchased From		$ per	____ct ____gm
Number Pieces		Total Cost	
Total Weight		Reference #	
Notes			

Date | Gem Species
Purchased From | $ per ____ct ____gm
Number Pieces | Total Cost
Total Weight | Reference #
Notes

Date | Gem Species
Purchased From | $ per ____ct ____gm
Number Pieces | Total Cost
Total Weight | Reference #
Notes

Date | Gem Species
Purchased From | $ per ____ct ____gm
Number Pieces | Total Cost
Total Weight | Reference #
Notes

Date | Gem Species
Purchased From | $ per ____ct ____gm
Number Pieces | Total Cost
Total Weight | Reference #
Notes

Date | Gem Species
Purchased From | $ per ____ct ____gm
Number Pieces | Total Cost
Total Weight | Reference #
Notes

Rough Catalog

Date		Gem Species	
Purchased From		$ per	____ct ____gm
Number Pieces		Total Cost	
Total Weight		Reference #	
Notes			

Date		Gem Species	
Purchased From		$ per	____ct ____gm
Number Pieces		Total Cost	
Total Weight		Reference #	
Notes			

Date		Gem Species	
Purchased From		$ per	____ct ____gm
Number Pieces		Total Cost	
Total Weight		Reference #	
Notes			

Date		Gem Species	
Purchased From		$ per	____ct ____gm
Number Pieces		Total Cost	
Total Weight		Reference #	
Notes			

Date		Gem Species	
Purchased From		$ per	____ct ____gm
Number Pieces		Total Cost	
Total Weight		Reference #	
Notes			

Date

Purchased From

Number Pieces

Total Weight

Notes

Gem Species

$ per ____ct ____gm

Total Cost

Reference #

Date

Purchased From

Number Pieces

Total Weight

Notes

Gem Species

$ per ____ct ____gm

Total Cost

Reference #

Date

Purchased From

Number Pieces

Total Weight

Notes

Gem Species

$ per ____ct ____gm

Total Cost

Reference #

Date

Purchased From

Number Pieces

Total Weight

Notes

Gem Species

$ per ____ct ____gm

Total Cost

Reference #

Date

Purchased From

Number Pieces

Total Weight

Notes

Gem Species

$ per ____ct ____gm

Total Cost

Reference #

Rough Catalog

Date		**Gem Species**	
Purchased From		**$ per**	____ct ____gm
Number Pieces		**Total Cost**	
Total Weight		**Reference #**	
Notes			

Date		**Gem Species**	
Purchased From		**$ per**	____ct ____gm
Number Pieces		**Total Cost**	
Total Weight		**Reference #**	
Notes			

Date		**Gem Species**	
Purchased From		**$ per**	____ct ____gm
Number Pieces		**Total Cost**	
Total Weight		**Reference #**	
Notes			

Date		**Gem Species**	
Purchased From		**$ per**	____ct ____gm
Number Pieces		**Total Cost**	
Total Weight		**Reference #**	
Notes			

Date		**Gem Species**	
Purchased From		**$ per**	____ct ____gm
Number Pieces		**Total Cost**	
Total Weight		**Reference #**	
Notes			

Date		Gem Species	
Purchased From		$ per	____ct ____gm
Number Pieces		Total Cost	
Total Weight		Reference #	
Notes			

Date		Gem Species	
Purchased From		$ per	____ct ____gm
Number Pieces		Total Cost	
Total Weight		Reference #	
Notes			

Date		Gem Species	
Purchased From		$ per	____ct ____gm
Number Pieces		Total Cost	
Total Weight		Reference #	
Notes			

Date		Gem Species	
Purchased From		$ per	____ct ____gm
Number Pieces		Total Cost	
Total Weight		Reference #	
Notes			

Date		Gem Species	
Purchased From		$ per	____ct ____gm
Number Pieces		Total Cost	
Total Weight		Reference #	
Notes			

Cut Gems Catalog

Date		**Gem Species**	
Shape		**Color**	
Weight		**Dimensions**	
Cut by		**Cost**	
Notes			

Date		**Gem Species**	
Shape		**Color**	
Weight		**Dimensions**	
Cut by		**Cost**	
Notes			

Date		**Gem Species**	
Shape		**Color**	
Weight		**Dimensions**	
Cut by		**Cost**	
Notes			

Date		**Gem Species**	
Shape		**Color**	
Weight		**Dimensions**	
Cut by		**Cost**	
Notes			

Date		**Gem Species**	
Shape		**Color**	
Weight		**Dimensions**	
Cut by		**Cost**	
Notes			

Date		Gem Species	
Shape		Color	
Weight		Dimensions	
Cut by		Cost	
Notes			

Date		Gem Species	
Shape		Color	
Weight		Dimensions	
Cut by		Cost	
Notes			

Date		Gem Species	
Shape		Color	
Weight		Dimensions	
Cut by		Cost	
Notes			

Date		Gem Species	
Shape		Color	
Weight		Dimensions	
Cut by		Cost	
Notes			

Date		Gem Species	
Shape		Color	
Weight		Dimensions	
Cut by		Cost	
Notes			

Cut Gems Catalog

Date		Gem Species	
Shape		Color	
Weight		Dimensions	
Cut by		Cost	
Notes			

Date		Gem Species	
Shape		Color	
Weight		Dimensions	
Cut by		Cost	
Notes			

Date		Gem Species	
Shape		Color	
Weight		Dimensions	
Cut by		Cost	
Notes			

Date		Gem Species	
Shape		Color	
Weight		Dimensions	
Cut by		Cost	
Notes			

Date		Gem Species	
Shape		Color	
Weight		Dimensions	
Cut by		Cost	
Notes			

Date		Gem Species	
Shape		Color	
Weight		Dimensions	
Cut by		Cost	
Notes			

Date		Gem Species	
Shape		Color	
Weight		Dimensions	
Cut by		Cost	
Notes			

Date		Gem Species	
Shape		Color	
Weight		Dimensions	
Cut by		Cost	
Notes			

Date		Gem Species	
Shape		Color	
Weight		Dimensions	
Cut by		Cost	
Notes			

Date		Gem Species	
Shape		Color	
Weight		Dimensions	
Cut by		Cost	
Notes			

Cut Gems Catalog

Date		**Gem Species**	
Shape		**Color**	
Weight		**Dimensions**	
Cut by		**Cost**	
Notes			

Date		**Gem Species**	
Shape		**Color**	
Weight		**Dimensions**	
Cut by		**Cost**	
Notes			

Date		**Gem Species**	
Shape		**Color**	
Weight		**Dimensions**	
Cut by		**Cost**	
Notes			

Date		**Gem Species**	
Shape		**Color**	
Weight		**Dimensions**	
Cut by		**Cost**	
Notes			

Date		**Gem Species**	
Shape		**Color**	
Weight		**Dimensions**	
Cut by		**Cost**	
Notes			

Date		Gem Species	
Shape		Color	
Weight		Dimensions	
Cut by		Cost	
Notes			

Date		Gem Species	
Shape		Color	
Weight		Dimensions	
Cut by		Cost	
Notes			

Date		Gem Species	
Shape		Color	
Weight		Dimensions	
Cut by		Cost	
Notes			

Date		Gem Species	
Shape		Color	
Weight		Dimensions	
Cut by		Cost	
Notes			

Date		Gem Species	
Shape		Color	
Weight		Dimensions	
Cut by		Cost	
Notes			

Cut Gems Catalog

Date		Gem Species	
Shape		Color	
Weight		Dimensions	
Cut by		Cost	
Notes			

Date		Gem Species	
Shape		Color	
Weight		Dimensions	
Cut by		Cost	
Notes			

Date		Gem Species	
Shape		Color	
Weight		Dimensions	
Cut by		Cost	
Notes			

Date		Gem Species	
Shape		Color	
Weight		Dimensions	
Cut by		Cost	
Notes			

Date		Gem Species	
Shape		Color	
Weight		Dimensions	
Cut by		Cost	
Notes			

Date		Gem Species	
Shape		Color	
Weight		Dimensions	
Cut by		Cost	
Notes			

Date		Gem Species	
Shape		Color	
Weight		Dimensions	
Cut by		Cost	
Notes			

Date		Gem Species	
Shape		Color	
Weight		Dimensions	
Cut by		Cost	
Notes			

Date		Gem Species	
Shape		Color	
Weight		Dimensions	
Cut by		Cost	
Notes			

Date		Gem Species	
Shape		Color	
Weight		Dimensions	
Cut by		Cost	
Notes			

Cut Gems Catalog

Date		Gem Species	
Shape		Color	
Weight		Dimensions	
Cut by		Cost	
Notes			

Date		Gem Species	
Shape		Color	
Weight		Dimensions	
Cut by		Cost	
Notes			

Date		Gem Species	
Shape		Color	
Weight		Dimensions	
Cut by		Cost	
Notes			

Date		Gem Species	
Shape		Color	
Weight		Dimensions	
Cut by		Cost	
Notes			

Date		Gem Species	
Shape		Color	
Weight		Dimensions	
Cut by		Cost	
Notes			

Date
Shape
Weight
Cut by
Notes

Gem Species
Color
Dimensions
Cost

Date
Shape
Weight
Cut by
Notes

Gem Species
Color
Dimensions
Cost

Date
Shape
Weight
Cut by
Notes

Gem Species
Color
Dimensions
Cost

Date
Shape
Weight
Cut by
Notes

Gem Species
Color
Dimensions
Cost

Date
Shape
Weight
Cut by
Notes

Gem Species
Color
Dimensions
Cost

Cut Gems Catalog

Date		Gem Species	
Shape		Color	
Weight		Dimensions	
Cut by		Cost	
Notes			

Date		Gem Species	
Shape		Color	
Weight		Dimensions	
Cut by		Cost	
Notes			

Date		Gem Species	
Shape		Color	
Weight		Dimensions	
Cut by		Cost	
Notes			

Date		Gem Species	
Shape		Color	
Weight		Dimensions	
Cut by		Cost	
Notes			

Date		Gem Species	
Shape		Color	
Weight		Dimensions	
Cut by		Cost	
Notes			

Date		Gem Species	
Shape		Color	
Weight		Dimensions	
Cut by		Cost	
Notes			

Date		Gem Species	
Shape		Color	
Weight		Dimensions	
Cut by		Cost	
Notes			

Date		Gem Species	
Shape		Color	
Weight		Dimensions	
Cut by		Cost	
Notes			

Date		Gem Species	
Shape		Color	
Weight		Dimensions	
Cut by		Cost	
Notes			

Date		Gem Species	
Shape		Color	
Weight		Dimensions	
Cut by		Cost	
Notes			

Cut Gems Catalog

Date		Gem Species	
Shape		Color	
Weight		Dimensions	
Cut by		Cost	
Notes			

Date		Gem Species	
Shape		Color	
Weight		Dimensions	
Cut by		Cost	
Notes			

Date		Gem Species	
Shape		Color	
Weight		Dimensions	
Cut by		Cost	
Notes			

Date		Gem Species	
Shape		Color	
Weight		Dimensions	
Cut by		Cost	
Notes			

Date		Gem Species	
Shape		Color	
Weight		Dimensions	
Cut by		Cost	
Notes			

Date		Gem Species	
Shape		Color	
Weight		Dimensions	
Cut by		Cost	
Notes			

Date		Gem Species	
Shape		Color	
Weight		Dimensions	
Cut by		Cost	
Notes			

Date		Gem Species	
Shape		Color	
Weight		Dimensions	
Cut by		Cost	
Notes			

Date		Gem Species	
Shape		Color	
Weight		Dimensions	
Cut by		Cost	
Notes			

Date		Gem Species	
Shape		Color	
Weight		Dimensions	
Cut by		Cost	
Notes			

Cut Gems Catalog

Date		**Gem Species**	
Shape		**Color**	
Weight		**Dimensions**	
Cut by		**Cost**	
Notes			

Date		**Gem Species**	
Shape		**Color**	
Weight		**Dimensions**	
Cut by		**Cost**	
Notes			

Date		**Gem Species**	
Shape		**Color**	
Weight		**Dimensions**	
Cut by		**Cost**	
Notes			

Date		**Gem Species**	
Shape		**Color**	
Weight		**Dimensions**	
Cut by		**Cost**	
Notes			

Date		**Gem Species**	
Shape		**Color**	
Weight		**Dimensions**	
Cut by		**Cost**	
Notes			

Date | Gem Species
Shape | Color
Weight | Dimensions
Cut by | Cost
Notes

Date | Gem Species
Shape | Color
Weight | Dimensions
Cut by | Cost
Notes

Date | Gem Species
Shape | Color
Weight | Dimensions
Cut by | Cost
Notes

Date | Gem Species
Shape | Color
Weight | Dimensions
Cut by | Cost
Notes

Date | Gem Species
Shape | Color
Weight | Dimensions
Cut by | Cost
Notes

Cut Gems Catalog

Date		Gem Species	
Shape		Color	
Weight		Dimensions	
Cut by		Cost	
Notes			

Date		Gem Species	
Shape		Color	
Weight		Dimensions	
Cut by		Cost	
Notes			

Date		Gem Species	
Shape		Color	
Weight		Dimensions	
Cut by		Cost	
Notes			

Date		Gem Species	
Shape		Color	
Weight		Dimensions	
Cut by		Cost	
Notes			

Date		Gem Species	
Shape		Color	
Weight		Dimensions	
Cut by		Cost	
Notes			

Date		Gem Species	
Shape		Color	
Weight		Dimensions	
Cut by		Cost	
Notes			

Date		Gem Species	
Shape		Color	
Weight		Dimensions	
Cut by		Cost	
Notes			

Date		Gem Species	
Shape		Color	
Weight		Dimensions	
Cut by		Cost	
Notes			

Date		Gem Species	
Shape		Color	
Weight		Dimensions	
Cut by		Cost	
Notes			

Date		Gem Species	
Shape		Color	
Weight		Dimensions	
Cut by		Cost	
Notes			

Cut Gems Catalog

Date		Gem Species	
Shape		Color	
Weight		Dimensions	
Cut by		Cost	
Notes			

Date		Gem Species	
Shape		Color	
Weight		Dimensions	
Cut by		Cost	
Notes			

Date		Gem Species	
Shape		Color	
Weight		Dimensions	
Cut by		Cost	
Notes			

Date		Gem Species	
Shape		Color	
Weight		Dimensions	
Cut by		Cost	
Notes			

Date		Gem Species	
Shape		Color	
Weight		Dimensions	
Cut by		Cost	
Notes			

Date | **Gem Species**
Shape | **Color**
Weight | **Dimensions**
Cut by | **Cost**
Notes

Date | **Gem Species**
Shape | **Color**
Weight | **Dimensions**
Cut by | **Cost**
Notes

Date | **Gem Species**
Shape | **Color**
Weight | **Dimensions**
Cut by | **Cost**
Notes

Date | **Gem Species**
Shape | **Color**
Weight | **Dimensions**
Cut by | **Cost**
Notes

Date | **Gem Species**
Shape | **Color**
Weight | **Dimensions**
Cut by | **Cost**
Notes

Notes

Notes

Notes

Notes

Notes

Notes

Notes

Notes

Acknowledgements

The author would like to thank all those who inspired and contributed to this book and its content. Special thanks to my faceting mentors, Will Smith (former USFG President) and Roger Dery, with whom I've shared many miles in Africa. I extend gratitude to all the USFG board members and volunteers who generously share their wisdom and time to teach the art of gemstone cutting. To those I've learned from, traveled with, and faceted alongside, including Kell Hymer, Boyd Fox, and Peter Torraca. To Doug Powell and Michael Holmess for your work in layout and design, and to everyone who contributed ideas and photographs. Extra special thanks to Kim, my wife of 40+ years, for putting up with me talking to (and sometimes yelling at) my faceting machine, taking trips to dig in the dirt, and letting me buy all those shiny rocks!